Citizenship and Social Policy

Nikos Kourachanis

Citizenship and Social Policy

From Post-War Development to Permanent Crisis

palgrave
macmillan

Nikos Kourachanis
Faculty of Social Policy
Panteion University
Athens, Greece

ISBN 978-3-030-59826-6 ISBN 978-3-030-59827-3 (eBook)
https://doi.org/10.1007/978-3-030-59827-3

This Palgrave Macmillan imprint is published by the registered company Springer Nature Switzerland AG.
The registered company address is: Gewerbestrasse 11, 6330 Cham, Switzerland

Acknowledgements

I would like to express my deep and sincere gratitude to Professor Dimitris Venieris, who taught me Social Policy, and to Professor Dionyssis Gravaris, who is still revealing me its critical methods.

Contents

CHAPTER 1

Introduction

This book provides a general essay on the relationship between particular constructions of social citizenship and particular forms of the welfare state, and the ways both have changed and evolved over time. The central argument is that the welfare state is an integral part of the capitalist state and, consequently, any structural changes in the latter will have a major impact on the texture and content of the former. This will be explored through a study of transformations in the concepts of social citizenship and the welfare state from the postwar period to the present.

In developing this thought it will be argued that, over time, these two concepts are moving towards a process of parallel transformations, with changes determined by the nature of the dominant political ideology and the structure of the economy and productive relations. By examining these parallel transformations we can distinguish various key parameters for understanding this relationship, such as the boundaries and conditions which shape these different historical forms of the social state. In this context, the transformations to citizenship lay the groundwork for the emergence of the rules that legitimize each individual historical form of the welfare state.

These reflections will be elaborated on by positing two different formulations of citizenship and the welfare state (with the latter being manifested in two differentiated grades of intensity). The first formulation is that of social citizenship and the postwar (or Keynesian) welfare state, while the second is that of the neoliberal welfare state. The first

N. Kourachanis, *Citizenship and Social Policy*,
https://doi.org/10.1007/978-3-030-59827-3_1

manifestation was that of active citizenship and the active welfare state. Subsequently, with the Great Recession of 2008, the formulation of the responsible citizen and the residualized welfare state (that is, a form that is geared towards a residual model of social policy) emerged. This phase, in the wake of the global financial crisis of 2008, legitimizes all the targets that had been systematically cultivated in a milder way in the first phase of the neoliberal welfare state. It aims at the liberalization of processes for the privatization of social policy and the shift towards a residual welfare state.

It is of particular importance that each of these periods is defined by the situation that succeeds it. The framework of the Keynesian welfare state becomes delineated shortly after its end, when the consequences of its delegitimization can be seen. Accordingly, the boundaries of the first phase of the neoliberal state can be discerned immediately after the start of the second (Great Recession of 2008). Each of these periods incorporates boundaries, rules of legitimacy, different forms and objects of intervention, and, of course, different interpretations and explanations. By way of example, Keynesian consensus was the legal basis for the development of the welfare state and social policy in the early postwar decades. Its purpose was to assist the state's macroeconomic intervention by pursuing a Keynesian economic policy and establishing a framework to support institutions for redistribution of income and rights.

For a variety of reasons this consensus can be derived from and shaped as a symptom of the general will. These different types of consensus are common, while the prevailing form of consensus over a given period of time is complex and dynamic (Gravaris 1997). Consensus evolves with continuities or discontinuities, with consent or conflict. Reasonably speaking then, the change in the measure of equilibrium to the sovereign will is a structural variable in the transformations of social citizenship and the welfare state.

Changes in such social formations and types of social intervention originate precisely from changes to these limits. In this sense, the Keynesian consensus was agreed between industrial capital and organized labor unions at a time when this could be justified. This outcome was not, however, static. On the contrary, this consensus coincided, according to Kalecki (1943), with a political-economic cycle that led to the redistribution of income and rights.

At the end of this cycle, the industrial class sought to recover whatever it had momentarily been forced to give up. This was accomplished through policies to reclaim the socialized processes of capital accumulation. In this second cycle (in this case, the neoliberal welfare state) there was a drastic restriction of income and rights redistribution processes and institutions (Gravaris 2018: 88–9). In this historical form, there was a reduction in the methods used by the state for the extraction of forms of social assistance that, until the advent of modernity, had been left to society (charity, mutual help, the social role of the church).

In the international scholarly literature there are several analyses of the relationship between citizenship and the welfare state for each of these historical periods separately (e.g. Marshall 1950; O'Connor 1973; Titmuss 1974; Pinker 1980; Pierson 1991, 2001; Turner 1997; Spicker 2000; Dean 2004, 2014; Clarke et al. 2007; Taylor-Gooby 2008; Hoxsey 2011; Dwyer and Wright 2014; Edmiston 2017). However, work that has attempted a macroscopic, parallel, and combined examination of these conceptual transformations is limited and does not always aim to fulfil such a purpose. In simple terms, the importance of the welfare state for transformations in citizenship has been little studied (Taylor-Gooby 2008: 7), although it is central.

A range of contributions to the international literature has attempted to study important aspects of this relationship. Christopher Pierson (1991) offers a key text on the emergence and development of welfare states and an introduction to their contemporary challenges. The classic study by George and Wilding (1994) deals with the main ideologies of welfare. O'Brien and Penna (1998) set out different theoretical approaches, which seek to interpret historical and contemporary changes to the welfare state. Fitzpatrick's (2001) book aspires to provide a comprehensive analysis of the theory of well-being. In particular, its Chap. 4 approaches citizenship as a complex set of obligations and rights, which is a crucial component of the theory of welfare. Deacon's (2002) study seeks to provide a detailed elaboration of ways of reshaping citizenship and social well-being in Britain and America. Dwyer's (2004) monograph is perhaps the most comprehensive reading of citizenship in the light of social policy, as it sets out a variety of different perceptions and versions of it.

Taylor's (2007) book attempts to codify the diversity of ideological approaches to the issue of well-being and to elaborate on the ways in which they are reflected in a range of social policies. The collective volume by Alcock et al. (2008) refers, in part, to the historical background and contemporary context of well-being and citizenship in Britain. Taylor-Gooby (2008) deals with the remodeling of the content of citizenship in light of the contemporary challenges facing welfare states.

Dwyer and Wright (2014) find that personalized conditions and obligations for the enjoyment of social benefits are now at the heart of the concept of citizenship in the twenty-first century. Edmiston (2017) points out that modern cuts in the British welfare state are undermining the effectiveness and universality of citizenship.

It is clear from this brief overview that, despite the existence of a significant number of studies that seek to relate the concepts of citizenship and the welfare state to a particular historical period, this is not applicable to a comparative assessment of the transformations to them between different historical phases. Efforts in the latter case appear to be extremely limited and it is worth mentioning two of them, which show evidence of convergence with the effort undertaken in this book.

The first is that of Ruth Lister (2011). Lister, in her attempt to highlight the context of the transition to what she calls the "era of responsibility," discusses the mild reforms undertaken by the Labour government in the United Kingdom before the Great Recession of 2008 and subsequently by the Cameron Conservative government. To do so, she examines the ways in which social policy measures have been used to create a treaty for social control and the promotion of citizens' responsibilities and obligations. Lister argues that this logic of "responsibility" was applied to the most vulnerable. As a matter of fact, increased obligations for access to social benefits have been introduced, as well as eligibility filters for fulfilling citizenship. In an environment like this, the state has created conditions of hostility to citizens' rights that, unlike increased responsibilities and obligations, are almost absent from the public agenda.

A second and more macroscopic effort is that of Moreno (2016), whose work contains the most relevant dimensions of the argument that will be developed in the following pages. Moreno argues that three different phases of the welfare state can be distinguished. The first is the golden age, corresponding to its postwar development. The second is the silver age, which was formed and evolved from the 1970s to the Great Recession of 2008. The third is the bronze age, which is unfolding in the current period of crisis. Through an analysis of each of the different periods that Moreno distinguishes, he concludes that the bronze age may well be the prelude to a return to a "prehistoric" social Europe.

Having focused on some of the central concerns of the relevant studies, this study then moves on to its central discussion. The originality of this work is that it attempts to examine the two concepts in their parallel evolutionary path. That is, after each theoretical analysis of the transformations of citizenship, this transformation is correlated with the form of the welfare state that has been legitimized. In order to achieve this ambitious and difficult goal, a definition of the methodological criteria used in the analysis is essential.

The way in which this book is structured (namely, first the discussion of the theoretical transformations of social citizenship and subsequently the discussion of the development of the welfare state) does not imply a one-dimensional, linear relationship. It is palpably not the case, for instance, that shifts in the understandings of citizenship come prior to institutional changes in welfare systems. These changes are more complicated. In this book they appear alongside and mutually reinforce each other. The reverse logic was also possible, namely of beginning each chapter with the institutional material (Keynesian, active and residualized welfare state) and then proceeding to an analysis of the changing understandings of citizenship as these developed alongside welfare state reforms. This would offer a more "applied" exploration of how welfare states have changed before getting to grips with how these changes have impacted on conceptual understandings of citizenship and, indeed, perceptions of how "we" view ourselves as citizens. The choice of presenting the theory first (social citizenship) and then the practice (the development of the welfare state) was done entirely to make it as easy as possible for readers to understand the two concepts.

To examine the two concepts in each separate historical period, certain analytical axes for their critical elaboration will be utilized. The first axis is the conceptual framework for analyzing the dominant, by period, version of citizenship and its critical appraisal. The second axis is the elaboration of the basic properties of the welfare state in these individual historical phases. The third and final axis is an overview and synthesis of the interpretations formulated by different theoretical approaches around the development and transformations of the welfare state. These horizontal dimensions of analysis will apply to the three different versions of citizenship and welfare state that will be considered. In other words, each of the substantive chapters begins with an overview of a particular perspective of citizenship before proceeding to critiques of that perspective and then to an examination of the particular form of welfare system (Keynesian, active and residualized welfare state), and understandings of it, that are associated with the conception of citizenship under review.

Schematically, as will be apparent from the forthcoming analysis, until the 1970s, the scholarly debate on citizenship and the welfare state was focused on the delimitation of decent living and the social participation of the industrialized citizen (male breadwinner). It was around this time that the grouping and classification of a first cycle of interpretative efforts around the development of the welfare state was completed.

From the 1980s until the Great Recession, scholars leaned heavily on those elements of political science that sought to study aspects of the recalibration of the welfare state (Pierson 1991). Despite its apparent retreat, the resilience of the welfare state was highlighted. The emergence of a discourse of new social risks and identities played a major role in these developments. Its prevalence coincided with the significant socioeconomic restructuring that was taking place in post-industrial societies. The individual actions of the citizen, through the cultivation of civic virtues and social policies was favored as a solution to the management of this new landscape (Petmesidou 2014: 16).

During the Great Recession of 2008, scholarly approaches focused on the processes and practices of state over-indebtedness, which attributed them to the increasing dominance of the international financial system and liberalized markets, fiscal derailment and the formation of a discourse that facilitated austerity measures and the deregulation of social protection systems.

The trend towards disintegrating and residualizing citizenship and the welfare state, as reflected in their dominant conceptual and political applications over the last five decades, raises major questions for the foreseeable future. This race to the bottom channels the dominant rationale for social management in the direction of a restoration of widespread poverty and social exclusion. Such conditions jeopardize social peace and, moreover, the functioning of democracy, which cannot fully exist without effective social rights.

References

Alcock, P., Erskine, A., & May, M. (Eds.). (2008). *The Blackwell Dictionary of Social Policy*. Oxford: Blackwell.

Clarke, J., Newman, J., Smith, N., Vidler, E., & Westmarland, L. (2007). *Creating Citizen–Consumers: Changing Publics and Changing Public Services*. London: Sage.

Deacon, A. (2002). *Perspectives on Welfare: Ideas, Ideology and Policy Debates*. Buckingham: Open University Press.

Dean, H. (Ed.). (2004). *The Ethics of Welfare: Human Rights, Dependency, and Responsibility*. Bristol: Policy Press.

Dean, H. (2014). A Post-Marshallian Conception of Global Social Citizenship. In E. Isin & P. Nyers (Eds.), *The Routledge Handbook of Global Citizenship Studies*. New York: Routledge.

Dwyer, P. (2004). *Understanding Social Citizenship*. Bristol: Policy Press.

Dwyer, P., & Wright, S. (2014). Universal Credit, Ubiquitous Conditionality and Its Implications for Social Citizenship. *Journal of Poverty and Social Justice, 22*(1), 27–35.

Edmiston, D. (2017). Welfare, Austerity and Social Citizenship in the UK. *Social Policy and Society, 16*(2). https://doi.org/10.1017/S1474746416000531.

Fitzpatrick, T. (2001). *Welfare Theory: An Introduction*. London: Palgrave Macmillan.

George, V., & Wilding, P. (1994). *Welfare and Ideology*. London: Prentice Hall and Harvester Wheatsheaf.

Gravaris, D. (1997). *Crisis of the Welfare State and Modernity*. Athens: Sakis Karagiorgas Foundation (in Greek).

Gravaris, D. (2018). Democracy and Social Policy in Times of Crisis—A Short Political and Economic Cycle. In C. Dimoulas & I. Kouzis (Eds.), *Crisis and Social Policy in Greece. Deadlocks and Solutions*. Athens: Topos (in Greek).

Hoxsey, D. (2011). Debating the Ghost of Marshall: A Critique of Citizenship. *Citizenship Studies, 15*(6–7), 915–932.

Kalecki, M. (1943). Political Aspects of Full Employment. *Political Quarterly, 14*(4), 322–330.

Lister, R. (2011). The Age of Responsibility: Social Policy and Citizenship in the Early 21st Century. *Social Policy Review, 23*, 63–84.

Marshall, T. H. (1950). *Citizenship and Social Class*. Cambridge: Cambridge University Press.

Moreno, L. (2016). Post-crisis and the Bronze Age of Welfare in Europe. *Working Paper*. Instituto de Políticas y Bienes Públicos (IPP) CSIC, Madrid.

O'Brien, M., & Penna, S. (1998). *Theorising Welfare. Enlightenment and Modern Society*. London: Sage.

O'Connor, J. (1973). *The Fiscal Crisis of the State*. New York: St. Martin's Press.

Petmesidou, M. (2014). Preface. From the Golden Age to the Age of Crisis. In G. Esping-Andersen, *The Three Worlds of Welfare Capitalism*. Athens: Topos (in Greek).

Pierson, C. (1991). *Beyond the Welfare State?: The new Political Economy of Welfare*. Cambridge: Polity Press.

Pierson, P. (Ed.). (2001). *The New Politics of the Welfare State*. Oxford: Oxford University Press.

Pinker, R. (1980). *The Idea of Welfare*. London: Heinemann.

Spicker, P. (2000). *Welfare State: A General Theory*. London: Sage.

Taylor, G. (2007). *Ideology and Welfare*. London: Palgrave Macmillan.

Taylor-Gooby, P. (2008). *Reframing Social Citizenship*. Oxford: Oxford University Press.
Titmuss, R. (1974). *Social Policy. An introduction*. London: Allen and Unwin.
Turner, B. (1997). Citizenship Studies: A General Theory. *Citizenship Studies*, *1*(1), 5–18.

CHAPTER 2

Citizenship and Social Policy: Conceptual Connections

2.1 Introduction

This chapter aims to clarify the meanings of citizenship and social policy and to offer an analysis of the relationship between them. The purpose of this is to develop a broader framework for elaborating the theoretical environment in which the evolutionary shaping of different historical forms of the citizenship and the welfare state can be understood.

Such an effort is associated with a series of difficulties that derive from the complex and pervasive nature of the two concepts. Both citizenship and social policy are interdisciplinary concepts that use (and are used) by a diverse series of social and human studies disciplines. An attempt to correlate them is therefore particularly demanding. Omissions and deficits can hardly be avoided. In the following pages, through a series of attempts to deepen the analysis, I will seek to elaborate on the content of citizenship and social policy, as well as the constituent element of the two concepts: social citizenship.

2.2 Citizenship

The concept of citizenship was revived in the late 1980s in Western scholarly literature as part of the wider context that saw the dynamic emergence of the role of civil society (Fitzpatrick 2001: 58). In simple terms, citizenship can be defined as "belonging" to a political community (Heater

N. Kourachanis, *Citizenship and Social Policy*,
https://doi.org/10.1007/978-3-030-59827-3_2

1999). From this perspective, citizenship is a vehicle for differentiation between citizens and people, building on practices of inclusion and exclusion. That is, who belongs to a political community is defined by those who do not (Wallerstein 2003).

The processes of including members of the political community and excluding non-members are largely shaped by the construction of criteria based on elements of social identity. Citizenship is interdependent with the sense of identity. The question of who is a member of a political community is a product of processes of delineation, meaning and the construction of principles, values and ideals (Alcock et al. 1997). The dominant identity largely determines the outline of the prevailing form of citizenship at any time (Fahrmeir 2007).

Consequently, it can be concluded that citizenship attribution is a dynamic phenomenon, since it depends on principles and values whose nature and character are by definition dynamic (Lister 1998). The constituent elements are political constructs, which are characterized by an inherent timeliness. Depending on the broader factors affecting citizenship, it is periodically associated with different forms of identity. If, for example, citizenship was primarily associated with class identities in the postwar era in Western Europe (Marshall 1950), then the dominance of neoliberalism from the 1970s onwards favored the promotion of cultural identities (Turner 1997; Ajani 2015).

Citizenship is thus a dynamic concept with multiple perspectives and, as such, it is extremely difficult to provide a clear definition of it (Cohen and Ghosh 2019). It is the result of the combination of different historical, economic, political, social, cultural and, of course, ideological developments, which together shape its multidimensional character. Citizenship involves power relations and conflicts between opposing ideological and political forces, which seek to impose their own political agenda on the historical phase of modernity.

It is to be expected that the diverse and dynamic nature of citizenship has been utilized by different disciplines of the social sciences. Law and political science, philosophy, sociology and other disciplines have borrowed elements of citizenship and developed them in different ways (e.g. Dummett 1976; Turner 1986; Kymlicka 2002; Milligan and Miller 1992; Kallio et al. 2016).

Different ways of using citizenship can be seen in Keith Faulks's 1998 typology. According to Faulks, the definition of citizenship incorporates at least three different types: legal, philosophical and sociopolitical. The legal type specifies the rights and obligations of citizens towards their nation-state. Usually the legal type takes the form of nationality. The philosophical type carries out regulatory and value processes around the pursuit of virtuous citizenry. Finally, the sociopolitical type refers to citizenship as a member of the wider political community, in which power relations are influenced by economic, political, social and cultural change (Faulks 1998).

The scholarly debate on citizenship has been divided primarily into two fundamental and methodologically inverse approaches: communitarian, which has its roots in the thought of Aristotle and the ancient Athenians; and liberal, coinciding with the emergence of modernity and the capitalist state. By implication, the communitarian approach focuses more on the obligations and duties of citizens towards their political community. The liberal approach emphasizes the dimension (individual, political and social) of the citizen (Alejandro 1989; Pufendorf 1991). The ideological manner of capturing the above two approaches does not have a complete impact on the real world. In practice, there is a mix of the two approaches and the proportions of each used is what determines whether citizenship in a political community will give greater weight to the rights of citizens or their obligations (Fitzpatrick 2001: 66–7).

The dynamic dimension of the two approaches also gives them a variety of shades and tendencies. The differentiated subcategories of the liberal approach place a different emphasis on individual, political and social rights. At this point, an endogenous divide can be formulated between the libertarian liberal approach and the egalitarian liberal approach to citizenship (indicatively Mthembu 2015).

The libertarian liberal approach advocates the protection and respect of a limited range of citizens' individual and political rights, with a primary focus on ensuring the smooth functioning of the market (e.g. Paul et al. 2005). In contrast to the libertarian approach, the egalitarian liberal approach argues that liberalism must incorporate a form of distributive justice with the aim of enabling every citizen to have equitable claims and respect for human rights. In order to ensure equal opportunities for all citizens, a necessary compensation for the persistent social inequalities produced and reproduced by the capitalist state is the addition of social rights to citizenship (Marshall 1950).

In the present work, the interdisciplinary concept of citizenship is approached from the perspective of its social dimension and, in particular, through the lens of social policy. The social rights dimension plays a crucial role in the relationship between the two concepts. The following are the main aspects of thinking around social citizenship.

2.3 Social Citizenship

The social dimension of citizenship is what guarantees access to welfare rights and resources to those who are considered members of a political community (Dwyer 2004), with the aim of their full participation (Marshall 1950). Similar to citizenship, the particular concept of social citizenship is highly dynamic in nature. Its dynamic content and orientations legitimize the physiognomy and priorities of social interventions attempted at each individual historical stage (e.g. Marshall 1950; Turner 1997; Lister 2011; Aasen et al. 2014; Gravaris 2018).

The main elements that have been intertwined with social citizenship to date, through different historical phases of modernity, are social class, gender, race, physical and mental health, religion, ecology, and a subnational, national and supranational delimitation of the political community as well as of cosmopolitanism (see for example Marshall 1950; Linklater 1998; Isin and Wood 1999; Dobrowolsky and Tastsoglou 2016; Pohlmann et al. 2013; Weithman 2006; Dobson 2003; Dannreuther and Hutchings 2016; Anderson and Hughes 2015). The dominant scholarly dialogue has concentrated on the prioritization of the class or cultural dimensions of inequality (Marshall 1950; Turner 1997; Tsoukalas 2010). This conflict arises from the aspirations of the dominant political ideology, as will be analyzed in the following chapters on the transformations and different versions of social citizenship.

These starting points indicate that social citizenship seeks not simply the respect and recognition of the dignity of citizens, regardless of their social status. On the contrary, it also implies the organization of a tangible set of institutions and services so as to eliminate a broad spectrum of forms of social discrimination (Turner 1993; Fraser and Gordon 1994). Citizenship, therefore, involves accepting the responsibility of the state to provide social support services to citizens (Wincott 2006).

The main vehicle for establishing the goals and values of citizenship is social rights. Social rights are that set of claims that seek to ensure decent living conditions and equal opportunities for citizens in society. They offer the façade of confronting the inequalities that are given birth to by the capitalist model of production (Titmuss 1958).

Social rights are seen as crucial to improving levels of welfare and legitimizing social support, in an effort to ensure equality and respect for human dignity (Dean 2015). They do so by legitimizing the removal of much of the welfare sphere from civil society and assuming responsibility for its founding in the functioning of state institutions (Offe 1984). A process with these characteristics has marked differences from that entailed by hierarchical relationships, which are usually consolidated by the practices and perceptions of the charity of non-state social actors. At the same time, it suppresses an acknowledgment of the social causes of inequality, which can only be mitigated through collective initiatives (George and Wilding 1994).

However, as has already been made clear from the analysis above, social rights are not universally accepted by all approaches to citizenship. Some versions, such as the libertarian liberal approach, advocate the safeguarding of citizens' individual and political rights only. In this sense, the recognition of social rights as part of citizenship is still at stake and has been significantly delayed when compared to the recognition of civil and political rights (Venieris 2013).

Furthermore, the exercise of social rights goes hand-in-hand with the fulfillment of obligations (Dahrendorf 1994). The measure of the balance between rights and obligations is critical to the potential impact of social rights (Dwyer 2000). The range of social rights obligations varies from country to country and is directly related to the wider structure and type of welfare regimes (Esping-Andersen 1990). For example, the social-democratic welfare regime seems less stringent in its interconnection of obligations and rights than the liberal one (George and Wilding 1994; Fitzpatrick 2001; Taylor 2007). The measure of the conditions around social rights determines the quality of the performance of social citizenship (Dahrendorf 1994; Venieris 2013).

The range of criteria for the enjoyment of social rights is largely determined by their decommodified or recommodified nature. The degree of declassification of part of the wealth produced to meet social needs, by virtue of the power of social rights, is reflected in the multiple criteria and conditions that are set (Adriaansens 1994; Kolberg 2019). The existence of criteria and conditions for citizens' access to welfare benefits discriminates between universal and selective social rights. This distinction, in turn, reflects a broader value-based intake of fundamental concepts, such as the principle of equality or the degree of need. In the version of universal social rights, all citizens enjoy access to equality-based welfare benefits. In contrast, selective social rights are confined to specific social groups based on the degree of social need identified by means-tested practices. At the same time, modern and more complex forms of social rights entitlement link access to social benefits with the fulfilment of individual obligations in a context of commercialized rights (Dwyer 2004: 10).

2.4 Social Policy

Social policy is the vehicle for embodying social rights as they transfer from being a constitutional requirement to an implemented social action. Social rights are the basis upon which social policy develops its interventions, as the dynamics of social policy development depend on the dynamics of social rights (Venieris 2013: 104, 114). In other words, the constitutional recognition of a social right does not automatically entail its implementation. Achieving the latter requires the recruitment of social policy (Popock 1992).

As with the concept of citizenship, social policy has dynamic and diverse characteristics. In the first attempts by its main academic founders to secure its interdisciplinary status, the definition of social policy was considered an extremely complex and difficult task (e.g. Abel-Smith 1958; Peacock 1960; Marshall 1965b). Characteristic is Richard Titmuss's caustic statement that "defining social policy is a difficult job" (1974: 28). At the same time, a fundamental controversy has been whether social policy is an autonomous scholarly discipline or the subset of another field of social sciences (Hill 1997).

Prominent scholars of social policy in the early decades were concerned with whether social policy could be autonomous as an object of the social sciences. For the most part, it was presented as a special aspect of sociology. For example, Robert Pinker described it in his writings as a sociology of ethics (Pinker 1974: 8–9), while the economist Peter Townsend disagreed with the separation of social policy from sociology (Townsend 1975: 1).

Nowadays, social policy is considered as an autonomous interdisciplinary subject of academic inquiry into social problems, which borrows tools and methods developed by other social science disciplines to shape its own existence. Thus, although it is a distinct scholarly discipline, it draws data from and builds relationships with other disciplines (Alcock et al. 1997: 7).

Reflections on the nature of social policy do not stop at its epistemological demarcation. On the contrary, they extend to its essential content. According to Marshall (1965b), social policy as a term can be widely used, but it cannot be clearly defined (Marshall 1965b: 11). Donnison sought to define social policy as embodying the social sciences in a practical/applied approach to solving social problems (Donnison 1975: 13). The above considerations can be considered justified if we consider a number of the changing and dynamic characteristics of social policy (Alcock et al. 1997: 7).

The maturation of the study of social policy and the more systematic attraction of a great deal of scholarly potential to engage with it has enabled its profile to be defined in much more certain terms (Venieris 2015). According to Dean (2006) the scientific object of social policy is the study of human well-being. This involves examining the social relationships that are considered necessary for social welfare and the social systems through which it is promoted (Dean 2006: 1). Spicker (1995) extended Donnison's (1975) approach to describe social policy as the study of social services and social welfare. Although the field of study may expand over time, engaging with social services is no longer at its core (Spicker 1995: 3).

A central feature of social policy is its dual nature (Venieris 2015). On the one hand, it is an interdisciplinary academic subject while on the other it is a term that refers to social action in the real world (Alcock et al. 1997: 7). At the academic level, social policy is approached as a vehicle for changing society (Titmuss 1968: 26). Titmuss emphasized the role of values and their influence on social action (Mishra 1989: 71; Deacon 2002: 14–26). Social policy is linked to values such as social justice (e.g. Hill 1996; Lister 2009), altruism (e.g. Deacon 2002: 14–26), the redistribution of resources (e.g. Peacock 1954; Abel-Smith and Townsend 1955; Abel-Smith 1964) and the alleviation of social inequalities (e.g., Abel-Smith 1966; Townsend 1979).

It is, therefore, an academic concept that, in all its areas of intervention, aims to achieve the provision of welfare (Marshall 1965a: 15). Hence, the study of social policy focuses on how social well-being is organized to meet individual and social needs for health care, housing, food, clothing and so on. Social policy is also interested in the ways in which social problems are recognized and resolved (Manning 1997: 31). It is a scientific term that deals with and interacts with the concepts of well-being, equality and freedom (Fitzpatrick 2001; Taylor 2007; Lister 2009), with ideological influences diffused within them (George and Wilding 1994).

Social policy as an applied social action is concerned with the planning, administration, implementation and evaluation of specialized state social services and local authorities. In the real world, the formulation of social policies often depends on political aspirations, political costs or the appeasement of the lower social classes. It is influenced and shaped by pressure from lobbyists and political conflicts. Often, the construction, hierarchy, and emergence of social problems are carried out in terms of political power rather than social needs (Edelman 1988). This is the other aspect of it, which usually goes hand-in-hand with rational and social control practices (Foucault 1980).

The scope and means of social policy implementation vary. Its main areas of intervention are social security, health, housing, education, employment and migration (Hill 1997; Alcock et al. 1997; Blakemore 2003). These fields constitute the largest part of any society's social protection system and aim to manage a wide range of social risks. The ways and means of implementing social policies also vary and they extend to three pillars of welfare provision: state, formal and informal civil society solidarity, and private.

Social policy, therefore, is comprised of two different aspects: academic study and applied social action. This duopoly also constitutes the essential contradiction of social policy: the attempt to balance academic values and political interests. It is a concept that constitutes, on the one hand, a scholarly object inspired by values and philosophical principles within the boundaries of utopia (Venieris 2006: 7), while on the other hand it is an applied policy that is attached to all the aims and interests of the political process (Cairney 2012).

References

Aasen, H. S., Gloppen, S., Magnussen, A. M., & Nilssen, E. (Eds.). (2014). *Juridification and Social Citizenship in the Welfare State*. Cheltenham: Edward Elgar Publishing.

Abel-Smith, B. (1958). Whose Welfare State? In N. Mackenzie (Ed.), *Conviction*. London: MacGibbon & Kee.

Abel-Smith, B. (1964). *Freedom in the Welfare State* (Fabian Tract 353). London: Fabian Society.

Abel-Smith, B. (1966). *Labour's Social Plans—Socialism Affluence* (Fabian Tract 369). London: Fabian Society.

Abel-Smith, B., & Townsend, P. (1955). *New Pensions for the Old* (Fabian Research Series No. 171). London: Fabian Publications Ltd.

Adriaansens, H. (1994). Citizenship, Work and Welfare. In B. van Steenbergen (Ed.), *The Condition of Citizenship*. London: Sage Publications.

Ajani, M. (2015). *Citizenship, the Self and the Other: Critical Discussions on Citizenship and How to Approach Religious and Cultural Difference*. Cambridge: Cambridge Scholars Publishing.

Alcock, P., Erskine, A., & May, M. (Eds.). (1997). *The Student's Companion to Social Policy*. Oxford: Blackwell Publishers.

Alejandro, R. (1989). *Hermeneutics and Citizenship: Critical Reflections on Contemporary Liberal Theory and Communitarian Narratives*. Unpublished PhD thesis, Princeton University, Princeton.

Anderson, B., & Hughes, V. (Eds.). (2015). *Citizenship and Its Others*. Houndmills, Basingstoke, Hampshire: Palgrave Macmillan.

Blakemore, K. (2003). *Social Policy: An Introduction*. Buckingham: Open University Press.

Cairney, P. (2012). *Understanding Public Policy*. Basingstoke: Palgrave Macmillan.

Cohen, E. F., & Ghosh, C. (2019). *Citizenship*. Cambridge: Polity Press.

Dahrendorf, R. (1994). The Changing Quality of Citizenship. In B. van Steenbergen (Ed.), *The Condition of Citizenship*. London: Sage Publications.

Dannreuther, R., & Hutchings, P. (2016). *Cosmopolitan Citizenship*. London: Palgrave Macmillan.

Deacon, A. (2002). *Perspectives on Welfare: Ideas, Ideology and Policy Debates*. Buckingham: Open University Press.

Dean, H. (2006). *Social Policy*. Cambridge: Polity Press.

Dean, H. (2015). *Social Rights and Human Welfare*. New York: Routledge.

Dobrowolsky, A., & Tastsoglou, E. (Eds.). (2016). *Women, Migration and Citizenship: Making Local, National and Transnational Connections*. Florence: Taylor & Francis.

Dobson, A. (2003). *Citizenship and the Environment*. Oxford: Oxford University Press.

Donnison, D. V. (1975). *Social Policy and Administration Revisited*. London: Unwin Hyman.

Dummett, A. (1976). *Citizenship and Nationality*. London: Runnymede Trust.

Dwyer, P. (2000). *Welfare Rights and Responsibilities: Contesting Social Citizenship*. Bristol: Policy Press.

Dwyer, P. (2004). *Understanding Social Citizenship*. Bristol: Policy Press.

Edelman, M. (1988). *Constructing the Political Spectacle*. Chicago: University of Chicago Press.

Esping-Andersen, G. (1990). *The Three Worlds of Welfare Capitalism*. Cambridge: Polity Press.

Fahrmeir, A. (2007). *Citizenship. The Rise and Fall of a Modern Concept*. Yale: Yale University Press.

Faulks, K. (1998). *Citizenship in Modern Britain*. Edinburg: Edinburg University Press.

Fitzpatrick, T. (2001). *Welfare Theory: An Introduction*. London: Palgrave Macmillan.

Foucault, M. (1980). *Power/Knowledge: Selected Interviews and Other Writings (1972–1977)*. New York: Pantheon Books.

Fraser, N., & Gordon, L. (1994). Civic Citizenship against Social Citizenship? On the Ideology of Contract-Versus-Charity. In B. van Steenbergen (Ed.), *The Condition of Citizenship*. London: Sage Publications.

George, V., & Wilding, P. (1994). *Welfare and Ideology*. London: Prentice Hall and Harvester Wheatsheaf.
Gravaris, D. (2018). Two Historical Forms of the Welfare State. In T. Sakellaropoulos, C. Economou, C. Skamnakis, & M. Angelaki (Eds.), *Social Policy*. Athens: Dionicos (in Greek).
Heater, D. (1999). *What is Citizenship*. Cambridge: Polity Press.
Hill, M. (1996). *Social Policy: A Comparative Analysis*. London: Prentice Hall and Harvester Wheatsheaf.
Hill, M. (1997). *Understanding Social Policy* (5th ed.). Oxford: Blackwell Publishers.
Isin, E., & Wood, P. (1999). *Citizenship and Identity*. London: Sage.
Kallio, K. P., Mills, S., & Skelton, T. (Eds.). (2016). *Politics, Citizenship and Rights*. Singapore: Springer Singapore.
Kolberg, J. E. (2019). *Between Work and Social Citizenship*. London: Routledge.
Kymlicka, W. (2002). *Contemporary Political Philosophy: An Introduction*. Oxford: Oxford University Press.
Linklater, A. (1998). Cosmopolitan Citizenship. *Citizenship Studies, 2*(1), 23–45.
Lister, R. (1998). *Citizenship: Feminist Perspectives*. Basingstoke: Macmillan.
Lister, R. (2009). *Poverty*. Reprinted Version. Cambridge: Polity Press.
Lister, R. (2011). The Age of Responsibility: Social Policy and Citizenship in the Early 21st Century. *Social Policy Review, 23*, 63–84.
Manning, N. (1997). Social Needs, Social Problems and Social Welfare. In P. Alcock, A. Erskine, & M. May (Eds.), *The Student's Companion to Social Policy*. Oxford: Blackwell.
Marshall, T. H. (1950). *Citizenship and Social Class*. Cambridge: Cambridge University Press.
Marshall, T. H. (1965a). The Right to Welfare. *The Sociological Review, 13*(3), 261–272.
Marshall, T. H. (1965b). *Social Policy*. London: Hutchinson University Library.
Milligan, D., & Miller, W. W. (1992). *Liberalism, Citizenship, and Autonomy*. Brookfield: Gower.
Mishra, R. (1989). The Academic Tradition of Social Policy: The Titmuss Years. In M. Bulmer, J. Lewis, & D. Piachaud (Eds.), *The Goals of Social Policy*. London: Unwin Hyman Ltd.
Mthembu, S. (2015). *The Individual and the State: Between Libertarianism and Egalitarian Liberalism*. Unpublished MA thesis, University of the Witwatersrand, Witwatersrand.
Offe, C. (1984). *Contradictions of the Welfare State*. Cambridge: MIT Press.
Paul, E. F., Miller, F. D., & Paul, J. (Eds.). (2005). *Natural Rights Liberalism from Locke to Nozick*. Cambridge: Cambridge University Press.
Peacock, A. (Ed.). (1954). *Income Redistribution and Social Policy*. New York: Macmillan.

Peacock, A. (1960). *The Welfare Society*. London: Liberal Publication Department.
Pinker, R. (1974). Social Policy and Social Justice. *Journal of Social Policy, 3*(1), 1–19.
Pohlmann, M., Lee, J. H., & Yang, J. (Eds.). (2013). *Citizenship and Migration in the Era of Globalization: The Flow of Migrants and the Perception of Citizenship in Asia and Europe*. Berlin, Heidelberg: Springer Berlin Heidelberg.
Popock, J. (1992). The Ideal of Citizenship since Classical Times. *Queens Quarterly, 99*(1), 35–55.
Pufendorf, S. (1991). *On the Duty of Man and Citizen according to Natural Law*. Cambridge: Cambridge University Press.
Spicker, P. (1995). *Social Policy. Themes and Approaches*. Edinburg: Prentice Hall.
Taylor, G. (2007). *Ideology and Welfare*. London: Palgrave Macmillan.
Titmuss, R. (1958). *Essays on 'the Welfare State'*. London: Allen and Unwin.
Titmuss, R. (1968). *Commitment to Welfare*. London: Allen and Unwin.
Titmuss, R. (1974). *Social Policy. An introduction*. London: Allen and Unwin.
Townsend, P. (1975). *Sociology and Social Policy*. Harmondsworth: Penguin.
Townsend, P. (1979). *Poverty in the United Kingdom*. Harmondsworth: Penguin.
Tsoukalas, C. (2010). *Inventing the Alternative. 'Identities' and 'Diversities' in the Age of Globalization*. Athens: Kastanioti (in Greek).
Turner, B. (1986). *Citizenship and Capitalism: The Debate over Reformism*. London: Allen and Unwin.
Turner, S. B. (1993). Contemporary Problems in the Theory of Citizenship. In S. B. Turner (Ed.), *Citizenship and Social Theory*. London: Sage Publications.
Turner, B. (1997). Citizenship Studies: A General Theory. *Citizenship Studies, 1*(1), 5–18.
Venieris, D. (2006). Limits of Social Policy. *International Conference*, Faculty of Social Policy. Panteion University, Athens (in Greek).
Venieris, D. (2013). *European Social Policy and Social Rights: The End of the Rapsody* (2nd ed.). Athens: Topos (in Greek).
Venieris, D. (2015). *Social Policy. Concepts and Relations* (p. 303). Athens: Topos (in Greek).
Wallerstein, I. (2003). Citizens All? Citizens Some! The Making of the Citizen. *Comparative Studies in Society and History, 45*, 650–679.
Weithman, P. J. (2006). *Religion and the Obligations of Citizenship*. Cambridge: Cambridge University Press.
Wincott, D. (2006). Social Policy and Social Citizenship: Britain's Welfare States. *Publius, 36*(1), 169–188.

CHAPTER 3

Social Citizenship and the Keynesian Welfare State

3.1 The Social Citizenship Approach

It is a fact that Thomas Humphrey Marshall's approach to citizenship has significantly influenced the relevant scholarly debate (e.g. King and Waldron 1988; Powell 2002; Turner 2009; Yalcin-Heckman 2011). Marshall is regarded by many scholars as the academic founder of social rights (Dwyer 2004). Through his interdisciplinary work—with a focus on sociological analysis—he was able to convince himself of the need to add the social dimension to citizenship.

Marshall's interdisciplinary lens stemmed from a wide and varied range of scholarly pursuits throughout his academic career. He began by studying economics, moved on to history, psychology and sociology and, at the end of his career, expanded to the discipline of social policy (Marshall 1965a, b). He was fascinated by a holistic approach to the social sciences, on the basis of which specific scholarly disciplines, such as economics, history, sociology, would interact fruitfully and effectively in order to solve society's problems. In a similar spirit, his thinking will be examined through his works on *Citizenship and Social Class* (1950), *The Right to Welfare* (1965a), *Social Policy* (1965b) and *Reflections on Power* (1969).

The starting point set by Marshall in his most popular work, *Citizenship and Social Class* (1950) was whether improving the living conditions of the working class has limits that cannot be exceeded. This research question sought primarily to diagnose and treat factors such as the arduous,

N. Kourachanis, *Citizenship and Social Policy*,
https://doi.org/10.1007/978-3-030-59827-3_3

heavy and time-consuming manual labor that deprives members of the working class of social participation. According to Marshall, the overwhelming burden of the working class prevented them from being educated and involved in the public sphere. It did not allow access to goods that until then were enjoyed only by the upper classes.

The workers were, therefore, trapped and reproduced their social position in conditions of poverty and strenuous work. In contrast, the higher-skilled workforce had better skills and more tools for critical analysis and an understanding of social events, but also more free time to further enhance these virtues. It had, that is, increased prospects for social mobility and improved living conditions. In other words, it had better opportunities for social participation.

Reducing the causes that impede the social participation of citizens is, in short, a fundamental parameter in Marshall's approach. This indicates that he was referring to a citizenship that stemmed from the citizen's active participation. His concept of citizenship involved citizens who, through their participation in the community, claim and achieve social gains. Social rights operate as counterbalances to those class parameters that prevent citizens from social participation. Social participation itself then helps citizens to safeguard and extend their social benefits. Social citizenship was, therefore, from the outset, a quality which required the active involvement and participation of citizens. This may, in itself, negate the foregoing criticism of the phenomena of passivity and welfare dependency associated with social benefits.

The importance of the political power of the citizen is deeply rooted in one of Marshall's later works, two decades later: *Reflections on Power* (Marshall 1969). In this, he analyzed the effects of the civil and political rights won in the eighteenth and nineteenth centuries through the forms of power that emerged in the twentieth century. According to Marshall, political rights fortify citizens by giving them political power. Through the exercise of their civil rights, citizens can influence and establish a system of enriched bourgeois democracy. After all, as will be seen in the development of his argument in *Citizenship and Social Class* (1950), the conquest of civil rights in the nineteenth century gave citizens the means to claim social rights in the twentieth century.

This active formulation and claiming through social participation would help the working class achieve better conditions for access to material and intellectual property. Technological development would provide greater scope for eliminating the physical strain of workers and an improvement in intellectual ability would offer every life the benefits and values of culture. These goods would enhance the prospect of public responsibility and social participation in general and enhance the prospects of turning the working class into "gentlemen" who can live dignified lives. For this reason, the state had to secure public expenditure to achieve this dual objective.

As regards the accessibility of tangible goods, Marshall considered it necessary to reduce working-class poverty to achieve this. The intensive and painful working conditions of the working class exacerbated the poverty of their living conditions. There should, therefore, be a humanization of work, with a focus on reducing stress in heavy occupations. Advances in technology would provide opportunities for improving the working conditions of workers. At the same time, this goal would also be fulfilled by the possibility of acquiring more tangible goods for those sections of the working class experiencing poverty.

The ability to improve the working class's intellectual abilities was to be achieved by one of the few forms of state coercion that Marshall included in his argument. The provision of compulsory public education to all children was a fundamental parameter of Marshalls' social citizenship. The enrollment of children into the education system was imperative in order to cultivate the foundations of a civilized citizen.

According to Marshall, helping with the first steps in life is a necessary condition for civilized citizens to then be able to choose their own paths later. The institution of education could ensure equality of social status; equality that would provide an equal starting point for the development of different life plans thereafter, based on each individual effort. The public education system would provide future citizens with the necessary skills of rational judgment and the ability to make rational choices as adult citizens.

The above discussion may help to clarify Marshall's own political and ideological orientation. His initial question as to whether there are limits to the possible improvement of workers' living conditions has created confusion around his ideological outlook. This is because a continuously improving standard of living for the working class has much in common with the political principles of social democracy. However, the equality of origin that comes from ensuring equal childhood educational opportunities for the creation of civilized citizens, which is indirectly referred to, demonstrates his liberal leanings (McKeever 2012).

There is still much evidence to suggest that Marshall's approach to citizenship was a liberal one, the most important being his analysis of the balance between economy and society. Marshall interpreted the relationship between economics and the social structure as dynamic; in other words, it was not a static, consolidated and unchanging situation. This is already clear from his emphasis on active citizenship and the demands of citizens, as well as on the linear development that he observed around the historical development of citizenship, as will be discussed below. According to Marshall, the problems of society could not be solved by purely economic or technical methods. On the contrary, the inclusion of social dynamics and the way institutions are shaped is intrinsic to the formulation of any policy that aims to address social inequalities.

Marshall differed with classical liberals such as Adam Smith in his views on the balance between the intervention of the state and the private sector. But this distancing did not in any way call into question the capitalist model. The functioning of the market and the reward of individual effort should be safeguarded, but without creating extreme inequalities that push the lives of citizens to the brink of misery. For Marshall, "abiding by market rules was a prerequisite for a just society." In other words, the inequalities caused by the functioning of the market were acceptable, but their scope should be regulated by the state on the basis of the prevailing social standards of living and the demands arising from the social participation of citizens.

Social policy itself should act as a stimulus for growth and contribute to the growth of economic wealth, as citizens with opportunities for social participation would have the capacity to multiply the production of material goods. In contrast to the earlier approaches of classical liberals, Marshall's case is that state intervention is a factor that contributes to the achievement of social cohesion and the expansion of the economic pie. Therefore, the addition of social rights to the concept of citizenship is something that enriches bourgeois democracy and stimulates the capitalist system.

Marshall's expanded approach to citizenship is also found in his work *The Right to Welfare* (1965a), based on a lecture he gave at Keele University in 1965. In this article, produced fifteen years after *Citizenship and Social Class*, the development of the postwar welfare state was seen as been the fruit of the long-term development of citizenship. For Marshall, it was a conscious choice to use the term welfare rather than "social services."

Marshall thus reiterates a holistic approach to the concept of rights as a whole. In terms of welfare, citizens' rights are interdependent and indivisible; they are equal. They are the links in a chain that lead, step-by-step, to welfare—a concept that lies somewhere between wealth and happiness. Citizens' rights are not, therefore, managerial-type social benefits for the alleviation of the symptoms of poverty. On the contrary, they are key factors in achieving welfare.

In developing his thought, Marshall ponders whether citizens' rights should be influenced by the design and conduct of social policy. Pointing to a series of historical examples, he concludes that access to social benefits or services must be above any technological and budgetary constraints. This does not mean that the use of a social service should be provided free of charge without the fulfillment of income criteria or the ability to pay of a citizen who is faced with a social problem. However, these costs may be covered by general taxation, social security contributions or, in some cases, part or all of the costs incurred by the citizen themselves. According to Marshall, the issue of the financial cost of social services is serious, but of secondary importance to the possibility of fulfilling the right to well-being.

Marshall's claim highlights an approach in which the safeguarding of rights is not trapped in a discourse on the constraints imposed by fiscal sustainability. This was indeed a factor that in the following decades turned out to be crucial for the conferring or otherwise of social benefits. On the contrary, in Marshall's view, the social services or social policy dimension is only one aspect of the right to welfare.

The origins of the right to welfare are deeply rooted in the whole socio-economic system. The achievement of this existential goal, therefore, goes far beyond the fulfillment of social rights. It relates to the enjoyment of other rights, such as the right to personal welfare, the right to freedom of expression, the right to choose and to exercise one's work, the protection of the citizen by the rule of law and more. Hence, it is no surprise that the dimension of welfare in the light of Marshall's work goes beyond the narrow limits of social benefits and touches on individual expressions of citizenship.

With a rationale like this, it could be argued that for Marshall social rights were a means to assist in the exercise of citizenship as a way of securing the basic conditions for the right to welfare. His ambitious working case in *Citizenship and Social Class* (1950) would thus be achieved (that is, by removing the barriers to excluding the working class from fulfilling social participation) through the compensatory benefits of social rights.

Adding social rights would complete citizenship, as it would lead to the prospect of living a civilized life in a cohesive society. Social rights would be the trigger for the enjoyment of social heritage: customs, morals, traditions, and the values of liberal democracy. The distribution of social heritage to all citizens was an essential prerequisite for being a full member of a political community, that is, a citizen. The momentum towards social cohesion would be the highest evolutionary stage of citizenship in modern times. Through the descriptive development of citizenship, Marshall sought to highlight the addition of social rights as a necessity for its completion.

Marshall's interdisciplinary training helped him select and utilize the appropriate scholarly tools for his analysis. Thus, although his argument has strong sociological foundations, his supporting argument draws on historical evidence. In his linear approach he distinguished citizenship into three equal and indivisible parts: the individual; the political; and the social. Each of these parts represents a set of rights. The first part (individual rights) is about individual freedoms. The second (political rights) relates to participation in the exercise of political power or the election of political representatives. The third (social rights) is concerned with the ability to guarantee a decent, civilized living and participation in the social heritage.

With a great effort at generalization and flexibility—and sometimes arbitrariness, which Marshall himself admits—he separated the evolution of citizenship into three different periods of modernity. Individual rights were founded in the eighteenth century. Their foundation was linked to the notion of an active subject and not merely one's freedom of consumption (Marshall 1969). Political rights in the nineteenth century paved the way for civil rights to be claimed by citizens. Social rights emerged hesitantly in the nineteenth century through the development of public education, but were fully won in the twentieth century, reflecting the modern social expression of the civilized citizen.

Until the twentieth century the impact of citizenship on social inequality was very limited. At this point, of course, the basic preconditions that had been established for the development of favorable conditions in which social citizenship could emerge must not be overlooked. The institutional framework for the protection of individual freedoms, but also the political power won by citizens through political rights, were important parameters in the pursuit of social rights.

As Marshall argues, the trigger for the revival of a social rights dialogue was the Charles Booth inquiry in the late nineteenth century. Booth's study was concerned with poverty and the living conditions of the working class, a reduction in income inequalities between workers and skilled workers, significant changes in the taxation of citizens, and expansion of the number of consumers of industrial products by including the working classes, who would have to have enough income to buy them.

A number of these and other similar developments have gradually led to the reduction of extreme inequalities and to the rise of certain aspects of social cohesion. This was a social cohesion that extended beyond the boundaries of the national idea or the values that belong to a political community. It was a social cohesion that rested on the foundations of the enjoyment of material goods by other social classes and not just the upper classes. The material dimension of social cohesion stimulated and enhanced the prospects of leading a civilized life for all citizens.

Until the twentieth century, social rights were not an element of citizenship. Marshall was convinced that they would be its natural evolution. Their addition meant a different understanding of the principle of equality. The theoretical conception of social cohesion would be translated into a practical response to solidarity while the manifestation of this solidarity would be about creating equal conditions for opportunities. Ensuring equal opportunities would limit inheritance rights and the reproduction of inequality on the basis of kinship and class background.

In other words, Marshall's Equal Opportunity Plan was formulated so as to create a common and equal starting point for all. Citizens would develop individual differences and inequalities based on their abilities and the efforts and choices they would make in their lives. The existence of such differentiations would not include extreme elements to the extent that they violated the possibility of living a civilized life. In this way, social citizenship could be a tool of social destratification (Marshall 1950).

The practical application of social rights is illustrated in *Social Policy*, a fourth work by T. H. Marshall (1965b). This monograph seeks an explanatory account of the development of the postwar welfare state in Great Britain. Starting in its first part with the founding of the first measures of state social policy at the end of the nineteenth century and up to the prewar period, it proceeds in the second part to an analysis of the British postwar welfare state until 1960. The analysis of the development of the postwar welfare state will be the subject of the next section.

3.2 Critics of the Social Citizenship Approach

Writing shortly after the disaster of World War II, Marshall attempted to make his own contribution to the debate on citizenship, which, in his argument, had been incomplete until then. Its completion required the addition of social rights next to individual and political rights in order to enable citizens to have combined access to all of them (Venieris 2013). Marshall's fundamental aim was to alleviate class inequalities through the distribution of the right to a minimum level of civilized living for all citizens (Holmwood 2000).

Equality of citizenship should be ensured, precisely because social class is an expression of inequality. The spectrum of class inequalities disrupts citizenship and, for this reason, the attachment of social rights to citizenship would redress the differences in equality of social status according to class origin. Simply put, the attachment of social rights would gradually shift the dimensions of citizens' lives from the parameter of social class to that of citizenship, from inequality to equality, or at least to an improved version with lesser inequality (Mead 1997: 198).

Fulfilling this plan would be achieved through the development of state social interventions by combining cash benefits (income transfers such as pensions or benefits) and benefits in kind (such as health, housing or education) that would protect citizens from the "adventures" of capitalism (Bulmer and Rees 1996). The process of decommodification played an important role in this policy plan (Polanyi 1944); that is, the reduction of citizens' dependence on market forces (Petmesidou 2014). Fulfilment of these interventions would result in citizenship impacting on social stratification (Esping-Andersen 1990) by enabling social participation for all citizens.

However, economic, technological and ideological changes in the years that followed led to criticisms of Marshall's approach. Some of these criticisms were influenced by the wider restructuring of the state since the mid-1970s. The impact of the first two changes (economic and technological) has been seen as crucial in the erosion of the postwar concept of social citizenship (Turner 2001: 189). Equally important, according to other scholars, was the third development, that of ideology (King and Waldron 1988: 416). These changes have resulted in Marshall's approach being widely questioned.

First of all, the Marshallian approach was accused of constructing a typology of linear evolutionary forms of rights (eighteenth-century individual rights, nineteenth-century political rights and twentieth-century social rights), which it sought to generalize. In fact, in some cases Marshall attempted to compress or ignore certain events so as to include them in the three categories of rights he considered necessary for citizenship (Fitzpatrick 2001: 61). Secondly, social rights were viewed as the highest evolutionary phase of rights, thus excluding the emergence of new forms of rights (Turner 2001: 203; Hoxsey 2011: 919). Third, Marshall attributed a one-dimensional—static—form to citizenship, ignoring the different types of citizenship that have developed in different nation states (Turner 1997: 15, 2009: 69).

Fourth, he did not sufficiently develop the dimension of the balance-of-rights measure (Yalcin-Heckman 2011: 434), an aspect that in practice can promote or annul the foundation of a social right. Fifth, a number of broader factors that influence the access and participation of vulnerable social groups in social rights, such as social status and employment, marital status and age, were not sufficiently taken into account (O'Connor 2002: 12). Finally, Marshall's Anglo-Saxon approach, with an emphasis on social class as a cause of inequality, led to the silencing of other forms of inequality due to cultural factors, such as gender, race or religion (Turner 1997: 13; Fitzpatrick 2001: 61). This broad range of criticisms has gone hand-in-hand with a shift in social citizenship from class to cultural inequalities and identities, but also to the emergence of active citizenship. These dimensions will be analyzed in Chap. 4.

3.3 The Development of the Keynesian Welfare State

Marshall argued that the real impact of social citizenship was the development of the welfare state (Dwyer 2004). Already from the late nineteenth century, several Western European countries had implemented certain early efforts to systematize social protection measures, through the establishment of social security systems (e.g. Perrin 1969). The most discussed example is that of Germany under Chancellor Otto von Bismarck (Kim 2007). However, the effects of World War II exacerbated social problems by expanding the need for wider state intervention to address them. This experience, as well as a number of other factors,[1] influenced the principles

[1] Factors such as the creation of nation-states, industrialization, urbanization, the commodification of labor, the struggles of the working class, the dissemination of collective val-

of social policy and the development of new methods of social management, ultimately leading to the emergence of the postwar welfare state (Marshall 1965b).

The choice of the term "welfare" implies precisely that the new social mission of the capitalist state is not exhausted in the painful relief of extreme poverty. Instead, its purpose is to organize a formal network of benefits to encourage welfare (Wilensky and Lebaux 1965), a concept which, both semantically and in terms of its orientation, could be considered similar to Marshall's (1950) civilized life.

In this new phase of the capitalist state, a range of social interventions focuses on workers and citizens. Social policies are designed and implemented to provide protection from a range of social problems (such as protection against the risk of old age, illness, disability, unemployment, poverty, homelessness, or for family support, etc.). This is also supported by the demands of organized groups such as political parties, trade unions, social organizations and, of course, the political power that offers citizens the right to vote (Sakellaropoulos 2018; Lipset 1960; Wright 2000).

The classic case of the development of the welfare state is that of the United Kingdom. Gradually (albeit individually for each country) the postwar welfare state was established and extended to other industrialized and economically developed Western European societies. This transition was financially linked to the general theory of employment of the economist John Maynard Keynes (1936) and politically to the report of the Fabian Lord William Beveridge (1942) (Titmuss 1974). Together, they formed the vehicle for building and fulfilling the "Golden Age" of the welfare state (Mishra 1984). This was the period when the perception that state intervention in the economy could be beneficial (Heald 1987) was becoming widespread, a period that extended from about 1945 to 1979. These two philosophies of the foundation of the postwar welfare state will be discussed separately below.

Keynes argued that in order to solve the problem of unemployment and to rebuild capitalist economies after the Wall Street crash of 1929, the state would have to intervene and create new jobs while financing the economy and business. The implementation of the Keynesian rule advocated the necessity of redistributing capital gains to the lower social classes

ues, the recognition of social rights as an integral part of citizenship (e.g., Venieris 2015: 94) and political rivalries during the Cold War contributed in different ways to the formation of the postwar welfare state.

in the form of social benefits. An increase in public spending in times of crisis could lead to a correction of the economic balance.

According to Keynes's theoretical scheme, the highest goal—economic growth—could be achieved by stimulating demand and creating full-time jobs, something that would be the responsibility of public policy institutions. In this context, the expansion of state activities in social areas served the process of development. This is because the social policy of the Keynesian plan itself could act as a factor for stimulating the economy by enhancing the income of the lower, weaker social strata as well as by mitigating class polarization and enhancing social cohesion (Keynes 1936).

The Beveridge report on social security and public benefit support services proposed reforms to tackle social risks. Published in the middle of World War II, it promised a reward for the sacrifices of the patriots in the war against Nazism. The Beveridge report was a central pillar for the implementation of the postwar welfare state in Great Britain. It proposed, among other things, the expansion of National Insurance and the creation of a universal health services (Beveridge 1942).

The postwar welfare state was built on the basis of the "Keynesian Consensus," that is, the convergence of the aims of the individual social partners for the legitimization and extension of state social intervention. The fundamental purpose of this consensus was to avoid situations of macroeconomic imbalance (for example, poverty, unemployment, etc.) and to remove the difficulties posed by the functioning of the private economy in the normality of social reproduction (Gravaris 1997). Within this consensus, a comprehensive network of insurance coverage combined with a broader set of social policies was proposed. The responsibility for regulating these interventions rested with the state as, according to this approach, its failure to fulfill them could be a source of social dysfunction (Kotsonopoulos 2016: 27).

The dominant perception of the postwar welfare state was, therefore, that the government had the collective responsibility for the well-being of the nation's citizens. This responsibility could not be delegated to individuals, private organizations or the local community (Mishra 1984). The adoption of social policy as a development factor favored its inclusion in the Keynesian political program. This was illustrated by promoting full-time employment along with the social benefits it provided as well as by establishing conditions to ensure a decent standard of living based on the living standards of each society (Cutler et al. 1986; Kotsonopoulos 2016).

This was a philosophy that was theoretically shielded by the Marshallian tenet of leading a civilized life.

Furthermore, during the first three decades of the postwar era, many areas of social policy were flourishing. Ensuring and protecting full employment and labor rights are two key developments of this period. The organization of work in the postwar welfare state was based on the Fordist accumulation regime, key features of which were mass production with vertical hierarchical control and full-time employment (Jessop 1991). Equally important was the development of an expanded framework of social benefits and services for protection against social risks (Johnson 1997).

Postwar social policy sought to ensure a minimum level of welfare (Venieris 2015), which was promoted by providing unemployment benefits, family benefits and supplementary income to those on low wages and old age pensioners. The welfare state also provided universal medical and education services as well as social housing. The main sources of funding for these services were state taxation and insurance (Pinker 1980).

In addition, the welfare state consolidated certain fundamental features, making it a historically identified form of organized social intervention by the capitalist state. Such features included the specific forms of income and wealth redistribution, the internal and external boundaries of the redistribution processes and the factor of social class in income and wealth redistribution (Gravaris 2018: 80–4).

With regard to the first point, in the postwar welfare state it can be observed that the redistribution of income takes place in an expanded and integrated form. This means that there are generous and extensive redistribution processes from the most affluent to the most vulnerable. The second subfeature is that of the institutional legitimization of this large-scale redistribution of resources at the level of government functions. Important in this regard are the concepts of social risk and decommodification.

The crystallization of the integrated institutional and operational recognition of the extended postwar redistribution process was embodied in the standardization of social risks. A number of different threats to a decent standard of living were regulated to provide protection through social policy interventions. The social problems mentioned above were addressedin the areas of the preventive (a social insurance system, usually funded by insurance contributions) or suppressive (a social assistance system funded by state general taxation) intervention of the social security system. The process of regulating these risks led to the indirect recognition of the state's social responsibility for the problems that citizens faced. The problems faced by citizens were, therefore, interpreted as being the social responsibility of the state.

The regulation of social risks was coupled with a widespread decommodification of the social benefits that are activated by them (Esping-Andersen 1990). If the concept of commodification is the process of converting material and immaterial goods into products of commercial value, then this concept may be understood as the degree to which there has been a reduction in the dependence of the standard of living of citizens on market forces (Petmesidou 2014).

According to Gravaris (2018: 80–4), the second dimension of the postwar welfare state lies in the limits of its redistributive processes. These limits concern the exogenous and endogenous environments of social policy. The exogenous environment is the broader context of public policy, in which social policy is shaped as government policy. The postwar period focused on the process of economic development, with an emphasis on industrialization, the generation of active demand, ensuring full employment and protecting the employment relationship. The Keynesian approach to the economy, as already mentioned, focused on fiscal policy and state regulation of the economy, as well as on the perception of the state as an employer in fulfilling macroeconomic objectives.

This spirit also affects the endogenous sphere of social policy, that is, the range of de-commodification processes and areas of social intervention. There is a public development of social interventions coupled with a widespread spirit of intergenerational solidarity (redistributive pension schemes) and the solidarity of workers (such as unemployment benefits with high rates of income replenishment), as well as of education as a form of social capital.

The third dimension is related to the social/class basis of redistribution. The redistributive processes of the postwar welfare state were closely linked to the social strengthening of trade unions and the working class, which was achieved through the consensus reached with employers. Ensuring a state of social peace and social dialogue through opposing social forces created a culture of neocorporatist consensus, which was particularly reflected in the institutional safeguarding of social rights. In this way, redistribution procedures corresponded to citizens' legitimate claims to the wealth generated, as well as to claims for decent living standards (Gravaris 2018: 80–4).

3.4 Interpretations of the Development of the Keynesian Welfare State

The diversity of interpretations of the development of the postwar welfare state highlights just how important this development was. In Sect. 3.3, numerous factors which contributed to the consolidation of social rights were discussed. There have been, mainly from the 1960s onwards, a number of different attempts to understand and justify the expansion of state functions in the social field with different scholarly and methodological tools (Pierson 1991). Functionalist and Marxist approaches, interpretations based in power resource theory, as well as explanations that use the scholarly tools of historical institutionalism have attempted to provide convincing interpretations of the development of social protection measures within capitalism.

A first set of approaches is rooted in functionalism and approaches the development of the welfare state as a mature need of society or the capitalist system. At least three sub-interpretations fall into this category: structural or functional approaches that emphasize, first, industrialization; second, the modernization of society; and, third, the needs of mature/advanced capitalism.

Interpretive approaches focusing on the factor of industrialization are the oldest. Since 1960, scholars such as Kerr (1960) have emphasized that industrialization means a new era for the world. For this reason, industrialization is defined as "the real path of transformation from rural to industrial society" (Kerr 1960: 14). The effects of industrialization on the detachment of individuals from rural societies from the practice of self-consumption and their transformation into industrial workers who sell their labor, the changes to outward informal forms of solidarity (such as the family), the changing demographic data and increasing life expectancy, as well as unfavorable living conditions in industrialized cities are the new social reality (Wilensky 1975; Petmesidou-Tsoulouvi 1992).

In addition, the proletarianization of the working class and, subsequently, the development of industrial workers' claims have contributed substantially to the assumption of social responsibility by the state (Thompson 1963). Several proponents of industrialization theories subsequently acknowledged the heterogeneity of the nations with welfare states, which attributed the changes in wealth surplus to the thresholds of economic growth, the long-term nature and resilience of the programs, and so on. (Flora and Alber 1981).

A second functional interpretation is one that uses the theoretical schema of the modernization of society to explain the development of the postwar welfare state (Rostow 1960). The theory of modernization has, in essence, four fundamental properties: the evolution of urban communities; the development of complex industrial processes; the attainment of a high standard of living; and the development of political and administrative systems (Hill 1980).

Modernization theory attributes the emergence of the welfare state to the increasing diversification of societies (differentiation of family and individual income, of living and working space, etc.), the evolution of citizenship from individual to political and subsequently to social rights, and the increasing control of the markets by the state bureaucracy. Moreover, it presents the consolidation of the welfare state as a by-product of political and social mobilization. This last parameter is reflected in the levels of industrialization and urban development, the mobilization of the working class, and constitutional structures (Flora and Alber 1981).

In the 1970s, Marxist-oriented approaches were revived, initially focusing on the needs of mature capitalism. Many such theorists, for example Rimlinger (1971), believe that the welfare state performs functions of social control in order to avoid social unrest. O'Connor's (1973) study of the fiscal crisis of the state was the first systematic Marxist interpretation of the welfare state. The state, according to O'Connor, performs two basic functions: first, it accumulates; and, second, it legalizes. In this sense, it seeks to secure the conditions in which capital can profitably be accumulated. However, if it makes overt use of its means of coercion to reinforce one ruling class at the expense of others, it risks losing its legitimacy or even being overthrown. For this reason, the state in mature capitalist societies reinforces the continuity, stability and efficiency of the economic system while ensuring the integration of social classes through social functioning. In this way, the postwar expansion of government spending helps to legitimize and safeguard the interests of (in this case, industrial) capital.

Other Marxist interpretations emphasize the political economy of the welfare state. In this regard, Gough's (1979) study argues that the capitalist state can never develop a range of policies aimed at truly meeting human needs. This is because policies with this philosophy will always run counter to the restrictions imposed by the profitability of the capitalist system. The development of the welfare state acts as an intervention that facilitates the process of reproducing the labor force and sustaining the non-working population. In a broader context, these activities can be linked to accumulation and legalization functions.

Offe (1984) points out that the postwar welfare state was established because earlier forms of social solidarity (family, church) could no longer meet the needs of the working class within urbanized society. The secularization process that coalesced with the evolution of modernity weakened the influence and power of the church. In addition, the extent of the social support provided by the family diminished as the commodification of the workforce expanded. The consolidation of the welfare state reinforced the process of the social reproduction of the working class and stimulated the productivity of industrialists. The postwar welfare state was therefore an indispensable precondition for mature capitalist societies. For this reason, Offe argues that it is a structural contradiction in modern political economy, since capitalism cannot coexist with social policy but it also cannot survive without it.

Other neo-Marxists, such as Quadagno (1987), argue that social protection programs do not have mature capitalism as their starting point. In fact, in some countries social protection programs have been traced back as far as the sixteenth century. What has occurred with the development of industrial capitalism is that we now also have corresponding levels of social protection. Thus, social policy programs within the postwar welfare state are expanded to respond to the processes and rhythms of industrial capitalism (Quadagno 1987).

A third category of interpretations derives its analytical tools from the power resource theory. This theory argues that the ratio of power distribution among the social classes is largely responsible for the successful or unsuccessful implementation of various political ideologies (Pierson 1991). This theoretical scheme has been applied to examine the development of social policy, in particular for the postwar period of advanced industrialization (Gregg and O'Connor 1998).

This approach argues that the political positions of actors with the power to influence decision-making processes play an important role in the development of the welfare state. In contrast with theories of industrialization, there is a great emphasis on the political dimension of events. Internal and external actors seek to impose their own goals and prioritize their own demands when shaping the political agenda (Rothstein et al. 2012). Mobilizing and organizing for the mass demands of the working class is a key factor in the social conquests won by capital (Wright 2000).

Walter Korpi's studies offer an important contribution to the development of this argument. According to Korpi, conflicts of interest between the social classes in the political arena of the welfare state can be seen as a form of democratic class struggle (Korpi 1983). There are two main sources of power: that of capital and that of the working class. The first source of power is that which has power in the field of economy while the second is the one that, based on collective demands, can maximize its political power and influence the redistribution of resources (Korpi 1980).

In this sense, the mass participation of working-class members in labor unions can enhance the effectiveness of social demands and lead to more generous social benefits. On the basis of such an assumption, the mass mobilization of the labor unions has strengthened the resource of the working class and, consequently, expanded social functions within the postwar welfare state (Korpi 1983, 1985).

According to the power resource theory, the degree of mobilization of working-class unions produces differences in the features of welfare states. This is due to the fluctuations in social benefits depending on the different political mobilizations and pressures being exercised in each state. This is most marked when parties of different political ideologies manage to retain power for a long time in different countries (Huber and Stephens 2001).

This observation triggered the identification and differentiation of different welfare regimes. Esping-Andersen attempted to use power resource theory to interpret the differences in development of different welfare state regimes. The ability and scope of the working class to mobilize, however, and the variations in its relations with the middle classes or the peasant class were an important factor for its effectiveness (Esping-Andersen 1985). In addition, the presence or otherwise of political consensus among government parties as well as the influence of the broader political context are crucial factors in the development of the postwar welfare state. This is also due to the inherent divergence among different families of welfare capitalism (Esping-Andersen 1990).

A fourth interpretative approach is that of historical institutionalism. Historical institutionalism leverages institutions in order to understand the evolutionary sequence of economic, political and social behaviors and their changes over time. In other words, it focuses on the study of the succession of events and especially those that are decisive for institutional change (Tilly 1984). Contrary to earlier theories that emphasized industrialization and capital, as well as the role of labor organizations, this approach focuses on the role of institutions and the reforms they undertake (Skocpol 1984).

In social policy terms, historical institutionalism attempts to examine the causal relationships in reforms to the economy and institutions that led to the formation of the welfare state (Lynch and Rhodes 2016). According to the dominant conception of this approach, the state has characteristics of social order autonomy. It therefore plays a central role in mediating social demands, in the evolution of socioeconomic processes, and in defining the boundaries for social reforms (Weir et al. 1988).

Mention must be made of a study by Theda Skocpol. Although Skocpol examines the development of social protection in the United States, which is not a typical example of the Keynesian welfare state, the theoretical and methodological tools she uses make her the most prominent representative of the historical institutionalism approach. In her 1992 book on the historical roots of the foundations of social policy in the United States, *Protecting Soldiers and Mothers: The Political Origins of Social Policy in the United States*, Skocpol sets four criteria for analysis: first, the processes of creating and transforming political parties and the state apparatus; second, the impact of political institutions and processes on the formation of the identities, competences and aspirations of social groups; third, the ability of these groups to adapt the access points allowed by the institutions; and fourth, the ways in which social policy trajectories are influenced by their future reforms (Skocpol 1992).

References

Beveridge Report. (1942). *Social Insurance and Allied Services.* London: HMSO.

Bulmer, M., & Rees, A. M. (1996). *Citizenship Today—The Contemporary Relevance of T.H. Marshall.* London: Routledge.

Cutler, T., Williams, K., & Williams, J. (1986). *Keynes, Beveridge and Beyond.* London: Routledge.

Dwyer, P. (2004). *Understanding Social Citizenship.* Bristol: Policy Press.

Esping-Andersen, G. (1985). Power and Distributional Regimes. *Politics and Society, 14*(2), 223–256.

Esping-Andersen, G. (1990). *The Three Worlds of Welfare Capitalism.* Cambridge: Polity Press.

Fitzpatrick, T. (2001). *Welfare Theory: An Introduction.* London: Palgrave Macmillan.

Flora, P., & Alber, J. (1981). Modernization, Democratization and the Development of Welfare States in Western Europe. In P. Flora (Ed.),

Development of Welfare States in Europe and America. New Brunswick: Transaction Publishers.
Gough, I. (1979). *The Political Economy of the Welfare State*. London: Palgrave Macmillan.
Gravaris, D. (1997). *Crisis of the Welfare State and Modernity*. Athens: Sakis Karagiorgas Foundation (in Greek).
Gravaris, D. (2018). Two Historical Forms of the Welfare State. In T. Sakellaropoulos, C. Economou, C. Skamnakis, & M. Angelaki (Eds.), *Social Policy*. Athens: Dionicos (in Greek).
Gregg, O., & O'Connor, J. (1998). Introduction. Understanding the Welfare State: Power Resources Theory and Its Critics. In J. O'Connor & O. Gregg (Eds.), *Power Resource Theory and the Welfare State. A Critical Approach*. Toronto: University of Toronto Press.
Heald, D. (1987). *Public Expenditure*. Oxford: Blackwell.
Hill, M. (1980). *Understanding Social Policy*. Oxford: Blackwell Publishers.
Holmwood, J. (2000). Three Pillars of Welfare State Theory: T.H. Marshall, Karl Polanyi and Alva Myrdal in Defence of the National Welfare State. *European Journal of Social Theory, 3*(1), 23–50.
Hoxsey, D. (2011). Debating the Ghost of Marshall: A Critique of Citizenship. *Citizenship Studies, 15*(6–7), 915–932.
Huber, E., & Stephens, J. D. (2001). *Development and Crisis of the Welfare State*. Chicago: The University of Chicago Press.
Jessop, B. (1991). Fordism and Post-Fordism. *Working Paper*. Lancaster Regionalism Group.
Johnson, N. (1997). State Welfare. In P. Alcock, A. Erskine, & M. May (Eds.), *The Student's Companion to Social Policy*. Malden, MA and Oxford: Blackwell Publishers.
Kerr, C. (1960). *Industrialism and Industrial Man: The Problems of Labour and Management in Economic Growth*. Cambridge: Harvard University Press.
Keynes, J. M. (1936). *General Theory of Employment, Interest, and Money*. London: Macmillan.
Kim, W. (2007). Social Insurance Expansion and Political Regime Dynamics in Europe, 1880–1945. *Social Science Quarterly, 88*(2), 494–514.
King, D., & Waldron, J. (1988). Citizenship, Social Citizenship and the Defence of Welfare Provision. *British Journal of Political Science, 18*(4), 415–443.
Korpi, W. (1980). Social Policy and Distributional Conflict in the Capitalist Democracies. A Preliminary Comparative Framework. *West European Politics, 3*(3), 296–316.
Korpi, W. (1983). *The Democratic Class Struggle*. London: Routledge & Kegan Paul.

Korpi, W. (1985). Power Resources Approach vs. Action and Conflict: On Casual and International Explanations in the Study of Power. *Sociological Theory, 3*(2), 31–45.

Kotsonopoulos, L. (2016). *The Lost Consensus. Welfare State, Capitalism and Democracy*. Athens: Sakis Karagiorgas Foundation (in Greek).

Lipset, S. M. (1960). *Political Man*. New York: Doubleday.

Lynch, J., & Rhodes, M. (2016). Historical Institutionalism and the Welfare State. In O. Fioretos, T. Falleti, & A. Sheingate (Eds.), *The Oxford Handbook of Historical Institutionalism*. Oxford: Oxford University Press.

Marshall, T. H. (1950). *Citizenship and Social Class*. Cambridge: Cambridge University Press.

Marshall, T. H. (1965a). The Right to Welfare. *The Sociological Review, 13*(3), 261–272.

Marshall, T. H. (1965b). *Social Policy*. London: Hutchinson University Library.

Marshall, T. H. (1969). Reflections on Power. *Sociology, 3*(2), 141–155.

McKeever, G. (2012). Social Citizenship and Social Security Fraud in the UK and Australia. *Social Policy and Administration, 46*(4), 465–482.

Mead, L. (1997). Citizenship and Social Policy: T.H. Marshall and Poverty. *Social Philosophy and Policy, 14*(2), 197–230.

Mishra, R. (1984). *The Welfare State in Crisis*. Hemel Hempstead: Harvester Wheatsheaf.

O'Connor, J. (1973). *The Fiscal Crisis of the State*. New York: St. Martin's Press.

O'Connor, J. (2002). Understanding the Welfare State and Welfare States: Theoretical Perspectives. In D. Baer (Ed.), *Political Sociology: Canadian Perspectives*. Oxford University Press.

Offe, C. (1984). *Contradictions of the Welfare State*. Cambridge: MIT Press.

Perrin, G. (1969). Reflections on Fifty Years of Social Security. *International Labour Review, 99*, 249–289.

Petmesidou, M. (2014). Preface. From the Golden Age to the Age of Crisis. In G. Esping-Andersen, *The Three Worlds of Welfare Capitalism*. Athens: Topos (in Greek).

Petmesidou-Tsoulouvi, M. (1992). *Social Inequalities and Social Policy*. Athens: Exantas (in Greek).

Pierson, C. (1991). *Beyond the Welfare State?: The new Political Economy of Welfare*. Cambridge: Polity Press.

Pinker, R. (1980). *The Idea of Welfare*. London: Heinemann.

Polanyi, K. (1944). *The Great Transformation*. Boston: Beacon Press.

Powell, M. (2002). The Hidden History of Social Citizenship. *Citizenship Studies, 6*(3), 229–244.

Quadagno, J. (1987). Theories of the Welfare State. *Annual Review of Sociology, 13*, 109–128.

Rimlinger, G. (1971). *Welfare Policy and Industrialization in Europe, America and Russia*. New York: Wiley.
Rostow, W. W. (1960). *The Stages of Economic Growth: A Non-communist Manifesto*. Cambridge: Cambridge University Press.
Rothstein, B., Samanni, M., & Teorell, J. (2012). Explaining the Welfare State: Power Resources vs. the Quality of Government. *European Political Science Review, 4*(1), 1–28.
Sakellaropoulos, T. (2018). Welfare State and Social Policy in a Historical Perspective. In T. Sakellaropoulos, C. Economou, C. Skamnakis, & M. Angelaki (Eds.), *Social Policy*. Athens: Dionicos (in Greek).
Skocpol, T. (1984). *Vision and Method in Historical Sociology*. New York: Cambridge University Press.
Skocpol, T. (1992). *Protecting Soldiers and Mothers: The Political Origins of Social Policy in the United States*. Cambridge: Harvard University Press.
Thompson, E. P. (1963). *The Making of the English Working Class*. Toronto: Penguin Books.
Tilly, C. (1984). *Big Structures, Large Processes, Huge Comparisons*. New York: Russell Sage Foundation.
Titmuss, R. (1974). *Social Policy. An introduction*. London: Allen and Unwin.
Turner, B. (1997). Citizenship Studies: A General Theory. *Citizenship Studies, 1*(1), 5–18.
Turner, B. (2001). The Erosion of Citizenship. *British Journal of Sociology, 52*(2), 189–209.
Turner, B. (2009). T.H. Marshall, Social Rights, and English National Identity. *Citizenship Studies, 13*(1), 65–73.
Venieris, D. (2013). *European Social Policy and Social Rights: The End of the Rapsody* (2nd ed.). Athens: Topos (in Greek).
Venieris, D. (2015). *Social Policy. Concepts and Relations* (p. 303). Athens: Topos (in Greek).
Weir, M., Orloff, A. S., & Skocpol, T. (Eds.). (1988). *The Politics of Social Policy in the United States*. Princeton: Princeton University Press.
Wilensky, H. (1975). *The Welfare State and Equality*. Berkley: University of California Press.
Wilensky, H., & Lebaux, C. (1965). *Industrial Society and Social Welfare*. New York: Free Press.
Wright, E. O. (2000). Working-Class Power, Capitalist-Class Interests and Class Compromise. *American Journal of Sociology, 105*(4), 957–1002.
Yalcin-Heckman, L. (2011). Introduction: Claiming Social Citizenship. *Citizenship Studies, 15*(3–4), 433–439.

CHAPTER 4

Active Citizenship and the Active Welfare State

4.1 The Active Citizenship Approach

The criticisms of the social citizenship approach, the ideological controversies around the welfare state in the 1970s, and the emergence of a discourse of new social risks, which will be discussed below, are associated with a gradual departure from the social citizenship model that was a political construct intertwined with the specific context of postwar welfare state development (Greenberg 1981). Its aim was the meaningful social integration of the industrial citizen, as part of a productive relationship that promoted full employment and a decommissioned version of labor and social rights, amongst other things (Esping-Andersen 1990).

The change in the cultural model of citizenship was determined by the rise of neoliberal ideology and favored by the transition to a post-industrial service society (Gilbert et al. 1992). In this environment a new version of the citizen, that of the active citizen, came to prominence. In response, the scholarly literature on the subject of active citizenship has flourished throughout the 1990s and the 2000s (Habermas 1994; Dwyer 2004).

At the heart of the active citizen approach is the notion that the sharing of common values of "belonging" to a political community and the consequent pride in shared local or national values, are to be seen as obligations. Active citizenship advocates that every citizen must be emancipated, autonomous, and flexible (Rose 1996). An active citizen is one who can shape his or her own career path by adapting to changes in the external

N. Kourachanis, *Citizenship and Social Policy*,
https://doi.org/10.1007/978-3-030-59827-3_4

environment. In this context, they must organize their life plan on the basis of their individual interests. Claiming responsibility for one's life and well-being is an individual responsibility (Jensen and Pfau-Effinger 2005).

Active citizenship is primarily concerned with the citizen's abilities, virtues and responsibilities, and secondarily with their rights. The ideal citizen is the one who makes the right decisions, is actively involved in the community, and takes initiatives that are socially beneficial. In this sense, active (virtuous) citizens must have a work ethic, contribute to the support of their families, and respect the rule of law and the rights of other citizens (Mead 1986).

On the basis of active citizenship, the right to welfare (Marshall 1965) is transformed into an "obligation" to work to ensure one's individual well-being. Consequently, access to social rights is increasingly intertwined with the aspect of employment (Gilbert 2012) while, in social policy terms, active citizenship is associated with a concept of "detachment" from state social benefits (Verhoeven and Tonkens 2013). Active citizens have a duty to take responsibility for their ability to be employable, to cover their health care, and secure a decent standard of living and their financial viability. Indeed, such a theoretical framework can also be considered favorable to the privatization of social services (Marinetto 2003).

The external (neoliberal) effects shaping active citizenship suggest that state responsibility must be strictly defined and residual, with the aim of managing extreme poverty. In essence, this approach recognizes social rights as an integral and indivisible part of citizenship, rather than as being individual and political (Dwyer 2004: 61). Inequality is seen as an accepted and vital condition of human nature. Efforts to deliberately reduce it are seen as an unacceptable situation that generates social distortions and negative side-effects. This observation has both class and cultural implications.

At the class level, the redistributive impact of social rights shrinks as the postwar objective of social cohesion is eliminated. The need to meet social needs is no longer an obligatory responsibility of the state and may instead be satisfied by civil society or the free market (Green 1997). The "Third Way" approach has played a key role in ushering in this spirit of social intervention.

The Third Way approach has in fact attempted to rebalance the share of citizens' rights to obligations by suggesting that the enjoyment of every right should be framed by the fulfilment of obligations (Giddens 1998). Although the Third Way acknowledges the central contribution that the public sector has to the ensuring of social rights, it is nevertheless vital for this approach that private sector intrusion into public social protection systems be considered. Access to social benefits can mainly be fulfilled through the labor market. The social rights of citizens who are unable to work are a secondary issue, as what is important is to enable and ensure the participation of the largest possible number of citizens in the labor market (Dwyer 2002: 274–5).

It is therefore understood that a rationale of active citizenship is to divide social rights. On the one side, there are the universal social rights of the social minimum, which are intended to ensure low levels of protection for the extremely poor. On the other side, a fully funded, mixed economy form of social rights is being constructed. These rights are customized in line with economic and labor data and, where appropriate, provide higher levels of protection for the strongest on the basis of these data (Venieris 2013).

At the forefront of this neoliberal drive is the removal of social rights from the notion of equality and from the principle of universality (Farnsworth and Irving 2011). Inevitably, their redistributive effect is replaced by a reciprocal relationship. Increasingly, social rights are linked to obligations and conditions, which most of the time usually fail to meet the needs of those citizens from the lower, weaker socioeconomic strata (Jessop 1993). The only concern shown for the weakest is in the creation of a residual network of social benefits for the management of extreme poverty (Rogne et al. 2009).

The contraction of state-provided social support, in line with the new dominant approach, is seen as "liberating" for those vulnerable groups whose survival depends on the welfare benefits provided by the state. By eliminating them, the beneficiaries will be forced to be active and seek ways of survival, notably through the labor market, the family and civil society solidarity networks (Murray 1984). Consequently, the state may confine itself to targeted repressive interventions for those who have already fallen below the poverty line and are trapped in poverty. Such interventions can also be undertaken by civil society or the market.

Active citizenship focuses primarily on social awareness practices rather than on activating the social protection system. Consequently, the question of voluntary work around social issues becomes central (Milligan and Fyfe 2005). These are the active citizens who must first look after and care for those with social problems. These developments bring to the fore the dimension of the role of non-state actors in the provision of social services (Wright et al. 2011: 299). In the area of social rights, therefore, the concept of voluntary giving to the community has returned (Gaynor 2011). To a large extent, this new political construct, as will be discussed in the next section, has been designed so as to help legitimize the process of European integration (Pfau-Effinger 2004).

At the cultural level, active citizenship seeks to read society in a pluralistic way and go beyond class inequalities, with a particular emphasis on cultural diversity. At the heart of this new version is the ability to recognize and accept diverse social identities (Turner 2001: 204). Most importantly, discrimination is not just about poverty. Social discrimination can come from the selective appeal to or stereotypical representation of members of society on the basis of factors such as gender, race, disability, ecological beliefs, etc.

Feminist perspectives, for example, have shown how citizenship was constructed in the postwar period according to a patriarchal logic. This form of citizenship did not sufficiently take into account the discrimination suffered by women due to the patriarchal structure of society. This can be considered as harmful to women, especially if one considers the significant contributions they have made to social struggles (Lister 1998). Citizenship should therefore be geared towards combating gender inequalities and better integrating women's needs (Pateman 2000; O'Connor 2002: 123–4).

The anti-racist perspective points out that citizenship, in the context of the national constitution carried out, has failed to remove racial inequalities (Brubaker 1992). It is therefore clear that citizenship must be directed towards more complex and differentiated approaches than on the basis of national identity, promoting multicultural practices and acceptance of diversity as well as combating cultural racism (Modood 1992).

Citizens with disabilities offer another perspective. This argues that the construction of social rights in the postwar context did not aid in mobilizing social groups for the disabled (Barnes and Mercer 2003) and so citizenship should therefore be reformulated to include disability (Dwyer 2004: 116). A final example is the ecological approach to citizenship, which seeks to link citizenship with the protection of the natural environment. This approach argues that citizens, as part of the natural world, must have an ecological consciousness and respect for the natural environment. They should also understand the impact of economics and technology on the ecological burden of the planet. In this sense, "green citizenship" focuses mainly on the obligations and duties of citizens (Dobson 2000: 41).

Given that economic inequalities are seen as something that can be acceptable for active citizens, the same then applies to cultural differences too. This occurs, however, through the same individualistic ideological and political prism: it entails coexistence within the social community while divergences from what is perceived as the norm are maintained. Any social intervention is used to ensure tolerance for the different and not to eliminate the inequalities that it causes through its interaction with the social structures of the socioeconomic system, a phenomenon that is evident in all individual manifestations.

However, the attachment to individual identities often works to the detriment of the solidarity dimension of rights (Venieris 2013). The holistic political programs of traditional ideological approaches are replaced by personalized identities, individualized demands of social movements that the dominant ideology shapes in its measure. These demands are made in a non-holistic and depoliticized spirit, demands that focus on individual issues of discrimination and inequality, largely disoriented by the parameter of the social order. This is a major element of T. H. Marshalls' approach. However, these demands highlight the multidimensional nature of social inequality. Paradoxically, in this way there arises the peculiar dilemma of the prioritization of social policy. The dilemma springs from the blurring of inequalities that stem from social class and inequalities that result from cultural discrimination, with a tendency for the former to be replaced by the latter (Fraser 1995, 2000), albeit with the same residualized spirit of social intervention.

The right of diversity recognition is therefore not excluded from social and ideological contexts. Perhaps the most significant development can be traced to the completion of the attempts at ideological individualization and its diffusion throughout the social sphere. Active citizenship, under the guise of neoliberal ideology, demands that individual identities be acknowledged through an instrumental approach. The "right to difference," a fundamental threat to all modern social groups that are subjected to the repression of what is allegedly "normal," and thus dominant, in terms of neoliberalism, is exploited by the powerful as the "right to inequality." The fact that the "right to diversity" seems to be detached from social justice and the right to immediate survival cannot, therefore, be regarded as accidental (Tsoukalas 2010).

4.2 Critics of the Active Citizenship Approach

Active citizenship dominated the 1980s and accompanied the restructuring of the welfare state (Jensen and Pfau-Effinger 2005), as will be discussed below. Its fundamental feature is that it again shifts the focus of attention from social structures to the individual citizen (Procacci 2001). At the heart of the approach is the citizen as subject, rather than the collective structures of which they are a derivative.

An essential part of active citizenship is that citizens must be active and take responsibilities (Newman and Tonkens 2011). Any arguments for active citizenship are exhausted through the ways in which they are activated so that they have the capacity to satisfy on their own social needs—largely through their employment. There is, therefore, a marked departure from the field of social rights, rights which are downgraded in the active citizenship version of citizenship (Mayer 2008).

Returning the focus of attention from social structures back to the actions and choices of citizens, in terms of their social rights, is linked to a shift in responsibility for social provision from the state to, again, individuals. It involves removing state institutions from the responsibility of providing adequate social living conditions. The phenomenon of the active citizen automatically shifts any obligation to ensure the well-being of the individual (Schmidtz and Goodin 1998). The active citizen must be trained, must seek employment opportunities and, through them, have the capacity to fulfill the conditions for access to the widest range of social rights (Blackburn 2008).

For those citizens who do not manage to become active, there is a residual social assistance framework aimed at the marginal management of extreme poverty. This is a low-quality social benefit framework designed to meet the minimum basic needs of the extremely poor; a framework over which there is no state monopoly. On the contrary, civil society and the private sector of the economy are involved in social initiatives by developing voluntary and socially responsible activities.

Active citizenship therefore has the effect of creating fragmented social rights. On the one hand, there is a residual network of social benefits, of a social assistance type, for the extremely poor. On the other hand, a range of reciprocal rights—of a fully funded nature—is being accumulated by those with the capacity for active citizenship and who have the opportunity to fulfill the—financial by nature—conditions attached to them. Such conditions are mainly related to their employment potential, but also to their employment itself (Venieris 2013).

Active citizenship also places great emphasis on the recognition and acceptance of diverse social identities (Turner 2001) as it is not just class that causes social inequality. Social discrimination stems from other factors too, such as gender, racial or ethnic origin, religion and so on. In this context, tolerance for diversity is a fundamental feature of active citizenship, and is the cornerstone for building multicultural societies. The acceptance and inclusion of diverse identities is the highest conclusive stage of active citizenship. Social interventions are depleted in the effort to eliminate racist and other stereotypes. Consequently, the very social subjects who have been accepted into the multicultural political community must as active citizens ensure their individual well-being.

The shift from social to active citizenship shapes a form of social rights that is less universal and less redistributive (Putnam 1993). Creating citizens who belong to different categories according to their abilities and choices disrupts social cohesion and increases the level of social inequalities, which it also legitimizes. The crowning point of this legitimization was the restructuring of the welfare state, as will be discussed below.

4.3 The Establishment of the Active Welfare State

The formation of active citizenship favored the rise of a broader environment in which structural changes to the philosophy and orientation of the European welfare states could take place. This plan was shaped by the ensuing political, ideological and socioeconomic developments (Johanssen and Hvinden 2013). The transition from an industrial model of social organization to a post-industrial society of services is the vehicle through which these fundamental changes have been achieved (Esping-Andersen 1999).

The abandonment of the Bretton Woods compromise and the collapse of the international fixed exchange rate system, the 1970s oil crisis and its effects on the economic downturn as well as other events that followed, called into question the Keynesian model of the welfare state (Gough 1980). A series of systemic developments focused on the political weakening of social democracy and the simultaneous promotion of neoliberalism, the globalization of the economy, the transformation of key social institutions, as well as criticism of social expenditures, combined to drive an argument against the principles of the postwar welfare state (Venieris 2015: 100).

The prevalence of neoliberal ideology from the 1980s onwards coincided with the revival of economic liberalism (Taylor-Gooby 1994). The aim was to reduce the levels and forms of state intervention that were popularized in the postwar period in Western societies. Because of this targeting, neoliberalism has been characterized by many scholars as a version of market fundamentalism (Heywood 2005).

Neoliberalism has saturated the process of economic globalization. The liberalization of international business, the development of the financial system, the digitization of the economy and the intensification of transnational money flows are key features of this complex phenomenon (Lemert 2016). The process of globalization has evolved faster due to significant technological development, and advances in new technologies have in particular helped to remove the barriers of time and space. Furthermore, the costs of handling information, people, goods and capital worldwide have dropped dramatically. This has enabled knowledge to become an important factor in production and development (Ramos 2003), as confirmed by its prioritization in the strategies of the EU (Copeland and Papadimitriou 2012).

This particular way in which globalization has developed has had a significant impact on the organization of work. The transition to a type of flexible accumulation replaced the Fordist model and ushered in the Post-Fordist model (Beynon and Nichols 2006). Post-Fordism has evolved into the new dynamic areas of the digital economy (such as telecommunications, automation, computers and energy). Flexibility in the labor market has had a major impact on the organization of employment: the dimensions attached to flexible accumulation were high-skilled workers, the growth of part-time jobs and the wider segmentation of the labor market (Harvey 2008).

All of these developments, which emerged in a schematic fashion, shaped the philosophy and characteristics of the neoliberal (or active) welfare state, which is highly critical of the Keynesian consensus (Pierson 1991). The active welfare state is based on certain positions that arise from a mixture of neoliberal and neo-conservative ideology. The synthesis of these positions forms a line of argument that is directly opposed to wider social intervention.

According to George and Wilding (1994: 21–35) the opposition of the New Right to the postwar welfare state is expressed in several points, which substantiate its positions on the residualization of social policy with the basic functions of individual activation and repressive care only for those citizens who are on the verge of poverty. A first assumption asserts that the goal of social cohesion affects one's spontaneous functioning. Social benefits trap the individual in limited choices, impeding their free development. Moreover, human nature is perceived as selfish and individuals seek to maximize their benefits. Therefore, the concept of social interest becomes impracticable as the aims of the social whole are in conflict. Every state attempt to link them generates more dysfunctions than social welfare provision.

A second argument concerns the mistaken perception that the supporters of the welfare state have of human nature in general. The New Right argues that increasing taxes leads to lower incomes and, by extension, causes people to become reluctant to be productive. In addition, the reduction in the sense of insecurity due to welfare benefits reduces the incentives to be productive. The concept of solidarity promoted by the philosophy of the welfare state is a form of illusion.

In addition, neoliberals argue that the welfare state has been based on a set of misconceptions and misunderstandings about the meaningful intake of welfare. The New Right interprets the development of the welfare state as the result of a misconception about the concept of freedom, the distortions of the concept of social justice, the perception of rights and the context of needs. Such examples for the New Right are the welfare state's emphasis on the aspects of equality and redistribution rather than wealth creation, the failure to recognize the importance of the right to individual choice, the state's monopoly over welfare mechanisms and other similar arguments.

Fourthly, neoliberals regard the welfare state as a threat to the fulfilment of the concept of freedom. Freedom is threatened by the ideas and functioning of the welfare state because of four main factors, the first being the traditionally expansive aspirations of governments. As the government inflates the public sector, individual liberty and individual responsibility are eroded. The second factor is the threat posed for freedom by the pursuit of equality. The New Right views equality as a form of coercive dependence, because redistribution naturally involves the element of coercion. A third reason that the welfare state threatens freedom is because it fails to offer individuals the right to choose, as it has a paternalistic and authoritarian role. For neoliberals, the market offers more effective forms of democracy by enabling everyone to make their own choices. The last point of the argument has to do with the organizational structure of the welfare state. There is a perception that monopoly organizations are dominated by strong bureaucratic and professional groups and the welfare state is a vital mechanism for reproducing such power groups. The New Right believes that the transfer of social benefits to market forces will give more power to consumers and less to bureaucrats.

For the foregoing, and for several other reasons, the New Right considers the welfare state inadequate and ineffective. Social policies tend to be implemented through large monopoly programs. With the lack of free competition there are no incentives for innovation or greater efficiency. There is again a reference to the point about bureaucrats and professionals in the welfare services, as rationalists seeking to maximize their individual benefits. Finally, the design, organization and implementation of social services conceal economic, social and political costs. Criticism is centered in particular on the firm belief that the free market is the essential driver of economic growth. Any intervention by the welfare state weakens and depletes the economy. Government spending on social services reduces the incentives for individuals to save and prosper (George and Wilding 1994: 21–35).

In the context of this widespread criticism, the properties analyzed for the Keynesian welfare state are to be adapted to the spirit of the new dominant ideology (Pierson 1991). According to Gravaris (2018: 84–90), these changes can be observed in the forms, limits, and the social/class basis of redistribution. The changes that take place are centered on the rationale behind the redistribution processes.

With regard to the forms of redistribution, a first major change relates to limiting it as a process, with a focus on shrinking redistribution to vulnerable social groups. Any redistributive process is adapted to (and largely exhausted in) the management of extreme poverty. A second important change relates to the resignification of the concept of social risk. Here, the processes of personalizing social risks play a key role, as illustrated by the transition from pay-as-you-go to fully-funded pension systems or the overlapping of unemployment benefits with the reciprocal utility work of the unemployed as a form of activation.

At the same time, a third characteristic of the forms of redistribution in the neoliberal welfare state is the new process of the recommodification of social benefits. They are acquired either as a product of the market or through the adequacy of the insurance contributions paid by each insured citizen. The sources of funding, namely the state budget, and the employment relationship still remain in the new environment, but with a reduced presence. State budget funding becomes limited, with the pretext of the financial crisis and later in order to reduce budget deficits. Funding from social insurance contributions is also limited because of rising unemployment rates and the reshaping of labor relations. The decline in these two sources of funding leaves free space and scope for private sector actions.

Changes within the redistribution threshold in the neoliberal welfare state internally relate to the breadth of the procedures for the recommodification of social benefits. They are also linked to the extent of the deregulation of the labor market, but also to the scope of the shift from "traditional" to new social risks. Externally, the limits of redistribution are in line with the model of state macroeconomic intervention. A key priority in the neoliberal welfare state is to regulate the monetary agglomeration of the economy with a significant level of freedom in individual markets. The consequence of this change is the transformation of fiscal policy as a tool to serve the purposes of monetary policy—and thus the abandonment of its redistributive functions—and the liberalization of markets by eliminating any factors that impede their free functioning. A tangible example of the new results that are produced is the abandonment of the macroeconomic policy objective of full employment.

Finally, significant changes are taking place to the social and class basis of redistribution. The typical features that suggest these shifts are the breaking of the consensus between industrial capital and labor unions, as well as the hegemony of financial capital. The first shift took place in two phases: the first was during the crisis of the 1970s, with the weakening of the trade unions and the subsequent convergence of social democracy with neoliberal authorities. The second phase began in the 1980s, with the adaptation of industrial capital to the logic of reproducing financial capital. It is this second phase that gave rise to the hegemony of financial capital. Key elements of this hegemony are the international liberalization of financial capital flows, the financialization of the economy and the intensification of competition at an international level. These changes have a strong impact on social policy, with the strengthening of private insurance companies and the expansion of the financial sector to the field of housing policy, etc. (Gravaris 2018: 84–90).

In addition, the chain of effects of the transition from the postwar welfare state to the active one is highlighted. The postwar welfare state relied on the Fordist model of production in a state-regulated national economy and with full-time employment and social rights as essential elements of productive relations and citizenship. The active welfare state became imbued with the philosophy of the Schumpeterian post-national workfare state. This version is dominated by the post-Fordist type of work organization with its dominant characteristics of flexibility and the transition to the service sector in an internationalized economy environment dominated by the national policy framework. In this type, social policy features are shaped by the needs of the labor market and the economy. They are provided in a mixed economy scheme with the basic requirement of fulfilling obligations to access social benefits, including workfare (Jessop 1993).

In the context of these structural restructurings that accompany the rise of the neoliberal welfare state, fundamental social rearrangements have taken place (Gilbert 2002). Significant cuts in social spending have resulted in the emergence of new poverty phenomena (Navarro 1998). Vulnerable social groups from the weaker socioeconomic strata that were not able to cope with the new economic pressures ended up destitute and dependent on social welfare benefits (Dean 2004). The one-dimensional focus of the dominant discourse of social policy on the new exceptionally excluded groups has resulted in the creation of a dichotomous construct: those who are within and those who are outside the "walls." The formulation of this discourse implied that the non-socially excluded body was unified, compact and homogeneous, while it silenced the multiple and significant inequalities within it (Levitas 1996).

The politically driven use of social exclusion has been transformed into a vital part of the neoliberal conception of the question of which groups are targeted for social interventions and how these are implemented (Byrne 2005: 57–8). The term social exclusion was initially identified with marginalized and morally dangerous groups, according to the thinking behind the philosophy of the underclass (Murray 1999). This particular way of portraying the extreme poor has attempted to reattribute the reasons for poverty from being ascribed to structural causes back to the individual again—to blame the poor for being poor.

In the decades that followed, the grounds for a more comprehensive restructuring of the philosophy of European welfare states was cultivated in a gentle, yet systematic, way through the process of social policy Europeanization. Strongly influenced by Giddens' Third Way approach and the slogan "No right without responsibility," it was considered imperative to establish a balance between rights and obligations. According to this view, social reforms had to form a residual safety net for non-workers and reciprocal social rights for workers. Cooperation between the state, civil society and the private sector could bring about the greatest possible efficacy in the provision of social goods and services (Giddens 1998).

The political construction of active citizenship and the emergence of active social policies have been the basis for legitimizing the European integration project (Pfau-Effinger 2004). The pervasive influence of neo-liberalism on the venture of European integration has promoted a spirit of residual social intervention (Preece 2009). At a time when EU economic policy decided to pursue a process of tight economic harmonization, in the field of social policy the mild adjustment of optional convergence was chosen (Geyer 2013). At the same time that economic policy was being subject to transnational decision-making, social policy remained a field for national intervention. This can be considered an example of double EU asymmetry (Scharpf 2002: 665).

For the implementation of the process for the convergence of Member States' social protection systems, the implementation of soft policy instruments, such as the Open Method of Coordination (OMC), was chosen (Sakellaropoulos and Berghman 2004). The application of OMC to social issues was first agreed in the Amsterdam Treaty 1997 on employment. Its wider implementation in the field of social protection was decided at the Lisbon Summit 2000. This promoted the mild nature of the implementation of Community policies in the field of social policy (Kvist and Saari 2007).

The attempted Europeanization of the Lisbon Strategy (2000–2010) has been extended to social inclusion policies, along with pensions and health. At the heart of the strategy was the transition to an "active welfare state," which would serve Europe's position in the knowledge economy. Key to this transition would be the development of labor market-oriented education and training policies, the development of active employment policies with improved employability and a lifelong learning priority. Also included in the areas of intervention was the modernization of social protection with a focus on an active welfare state that ensured economic efficiency, social inclusion, gender equality and the provision of quality health services (Feronas 2013).

The Lisbon Strategy was built on highly economy-centered foundations with the main goal of achieving growth (Kröger 2009); all the Lisbon goals aimed to achieve growth (Natali 2010: 14). With this in mind, any intervention in the social field was aimed at reducing social costs in order to ensure the economic viability of social protection systems (Geyer 2013). The establishment of active social policies (Bonoli 2013) reflects the prevalence of the individual over the collective. New active forms of social policy are intertwined with re-commodified, reciprocal and individual-centered aspects of social rights (Venieris 2013: 467).

Characteristic in these transformations is the current trend of transition from pay-as-you-go to fully funded pensions systems. This is a departure from insurance schemes that promote intergenerational solidarity to systems in which the level of pension and insurance benefits an individual receives depends on their job position and the length of their working life. Such systems exacerbate the phenomenon of lack of insurance coverage and of underinsured citizens (Frericks 2011: 319). In this new landscape, only one type of pension coverage, below the poverty line, contains elements of universality.

In addition, the Lisbon Strategy encouraged a multiplicity of social interventions from different welfare pillars. Simply put, the state is not the sole provider of social policy. International organizations, local authorities, NGOs, charities, grassroots initiatives and large private companies can be involved and assume social responsibilities. The Lisbon Strategy favored the shift in responsibility for the fulfillment of social rights from the state to civil society.

Analyses by political scientists have shown since the 1970s that the concentration of power in the state coincides with the accumulation of political costs in governments. The decentralization of responsibilities results in the sharing of political costs among many actors but also an increase in the number of actors, which may hinder policy implementation (Lowi 1972). Therefore, the process of the privatization of social policy—both at the supranational (European integration) and subnational (local authorities, civil society) level—could also be understood as an attempt to mitigate the political costs of national governments in the context of promoting neoliberal reforms.

The most typical example of transferring state social policy to decentralized institutions is the prevalence of the concept of welfare pluralism (Ferrera and Hemerijck 2003). Welfare pluralism argues that welfare can be offered by pillars other than the state (Johnson 2014). A number of institutions, such as the informal family protection network, wider civil society, and even the private sector, through corporate social responsibility practices, can complement or autonomously contribute to the provision of welfare (Alcock et al. 1997). The Lisbon Strategy encouraged their involvement and participation by making them equal players in the implementation of social policies.

Finally, the Lisbon Strategy formalized the spirit of minimal intervention to tackle the most extreme manifestations of social problems. The political adoption of the term "social exclusion" essentially implied a focus solely on combating extreme social inequalities (Levitas 1996). At the same time, the replacement of the economically centered concept of poverty with that of social exclusion effectively led a shift away from a class perspective of inequalities. The expansion of social interventions and actions to eradicate cultural discrimination (racial, gender, religious, etc.) came under the guidance of a toolkit imbued with the dominant ideological perspective of neoliberalism (Tsoukalas 2010).

4.4 Interpretations of the Development of the Active Welfare State

The crisis of the Keynesian welfare state and its succession by the active/neoliberal welfare state coincided with structural shifts in the philosophy and spirit of citizenship and social policy. These developments have been interpreted by different schools of thought through the application of their own scientific tools. Three different interpretative approaches will be discussed below: the approach to post-industrial society and the new social risks; the new institutional approach; and later versions of power resources theory with an emphasis on the role of enterprises.

A large body of interpretations comes from scholars who argue that social policy restructuring is due to the economic, political, social and cultural developments that took place after the early postwar decades. These developments have led to post-industrial society and the emergence of new social risks arising from it. According to Taylor-Gooby (2004: 2), new social risks are the risks that people face today during their lives as a result of the economic and social changes associated with the transition to a post-industrial society.

The dynamics of globalization and the transition from an industrial to a post-industrial society, widespread changes in family structure and gender relations, but also the long period of economic recession, high unemployment and the transition to an aging demographic trend have created a very different climate from that of the early postwar decades. This interpretation holds that since the 1980s it is not only significant cuts in the social spending of welfare states that can be observed, but structural rearrangements are also taking place, to adapt to the range of new social risks (Myles and Quadagno 2002).

The process of economic globalization is seen as a structural parameter that changes the profile of the postwar welfare state. The internationalization of the economy strengthens the negotiating power of world capital, thereby overturning the equilibrium of the postwar trade union consensus (Carnoy et al. 1993). Economic elites are more likely to move their businesses to countries that are more economically profitable due to lower taxation, lower wage costs or limited social policies (Mishra 1999) and the main victims of this development are national social protection systems, which are at risk of social dumping (Bernaciak 2012).

A second interpretation of the new social risks is the process of the transition from an industrial to a post-industrial society. The structural transformations that have occurred in manufacturing processes with the shift from manufacturing industry to the tertiary service sector have contributed significantly to the restructuring of the welfare state (Gilbert et al. 1992).

This transition is also accompanied by a reduction in blue collar workers and, by extension, a weakening of the labor movement. The political role of trade unions and workers' claims were important parameters for the social conquests that were founded on the concept of social citizenship. Consequently, the weakening of the trade unions has led to a reduction in the decommodified benefits that were based on the industrial citizen model (Jensen and Pfau-Effinger 2005). This was aided by the introduction of flexibility as a key feature of the new way of organizing work (Gilbert et al. 1992). The inadequacy of the service sector to create increased and organized productivity, compared to the postwar industrial standard, leads to the inability to cope with the resulting changes (Iversen and Wren 1998). In addition, significant problems can be observed for young people attempting to enter the labor market for the first time, but also in maintaining stable and secure jobs (Taylor-Gooby 2004).

An additional constituent of the range of new social risks is changes in family patterns and gender relations. The model of the industrial citizen was strongly attached to the male breadwinner philosophy. The convergence of post-industrial society with the tertiary service sector enables a higher proportion of women to be employed (Esping-Andersen 1999). The entry of more women into the labor market creates new social needs, such as the care of children and the elderly (Walby 1994). At the same time, the fact of women working outside the home and changes in family patterns create the need for additional social support measures for growing numbers of single-parent families (Rubery 1999).

The phenomenon of demographic aging is an equally important dimension of new social risks (Ferrera and Rhodes 2000). The decrease in fertility levels coupled with the increase in life expectancy puts pressure on key parameters of social protection systems with a primary focus on pensions (Jackson 1998). This, among other things, favors the shift from redistributive pension schemes focusing on intergenerational solidarity to funded pension schemes focusing on personalization of insurance liability (Rogne et al. 2009).

A second major category that seeks to interpret the transition to the active welfare state is the neo-institutional approach. Such interpretations are considered successors of the historical institutionalism approach discussed in Chap. 3. The emergence of neo-institutionalism is attributed to radical sociopolitical developments, such as the acceleration of the globalization process, the consolidation of neoliberalism and the emergence of a range of new social risks in post-industrial society (Kotsonopoulos 2016: 157).

The neoinstitutional approach examines how institutions influence each other and their impact on social organization. In other words, institutions shape the evolution of political and social processes and within this context they themselves evolve and transform (March and Olsen 1984). The neoinstitutional approach goes beyond the economic parameter as a framework for interpretation and seeks to explain the emerging forms and the role of institutions in every social environment (Powell and Dimaggio 1991).

According to neoinstitutionalism, significant changes, such as those mentioned in the previous paragraph, weakened the role of the state and therefore the focus was on the functioning and parameter of the broader institutions in the exercise of public policy rather than exclusively on the dimension of the state (Peters 2019). Despite the decline of the role of the state, social benefits have been affected, but they have shown relative resilience and have not been completely eliminated. This has led many scholars to attempt to explain these political dynamics (Starke 2006).

The most important representative of this approach is Paul Pierson. Pierson argued that despite the significant neoliberal reforms that took place in the 1980s, social benefits have shown resilience. His attempt to interpret this leverages the fundamental tools of the historical institutionalism approach, such as the path dependence of reform. In interpreting the resilience of welfare mechanisms, he develops a theory of the new politics of the welfare state. According to Pierson, the postwar expansion of the welfare state may have reversed, but historical dependence has resulted in the resilience of social protection mechanisms. Therefore, while there may be a tendency for social policies to shrink, this is not the case in all areas.

Pierson shapes his interpretation of the resilience of the welfare state around two central axes. First, his research overview highlights the persistence of core social benefits and institutions in Western countries. This is indeed very high up on the political agenda. Consequently, the more attempts that are made to limit social spending, the greater the political cost to governments. For this reason, governments attempt to avoid being blamed for what happens to the welfare state while they are in power (Pierson 1994, 2001; Starke 2006). The thirty-year postwar golden age of the welfare state generated various forms of powerful interest groups (e.g. pension lobbies), which are ready to mobilize and resist any venture that is against their own interests.

The second key element in Pierson's analysis is the historical imprint of institutional development. Many institutions—notably those that had a role in the deep-rooted establishment of the welfare state—have inherent dysfunctions. Their change must therefore be gentle and aim at reform, while any attempt at gradual change must coexist with the existing social policy framework.

These two axes lead Pierson to claim that politicians seek to avoid radical and outrageous cuts in social spending precisely because of their high political cost. They therefore seek to avoid responsibility for such political choices. Consequently, because of these institutional dependencies, the end of the welfare state, at least in the medium term, is avoided (Starke 2006).

A fourth interpretative approach to restructuring the welfare state comes from different versions of power resources. In contrast to the emphasis placed on the influence of trade unions and wider left-wing organizations in building a postwar welfare state, subsequent attempts to explain change focus on the role of businesses and employers (Swenson 2002; Hacker and Pierson 2002).

For many scholars, the development of the welfare state has been one that is compatible with profitability and business interests (Swenson 2002). Particularly where production processes required the existence of a skilled workforce, employers encouraged the development of the welfare state (Korpi 2006). Indeed, the approach that focuses on the diversity of capitalism holds that the different levels of employers' needs for more-or-less skilled labor has produced the differences between different national economies and welfare states (Hall and Soskice 2001).

An important contemporary variable in the understanding of this approach is the changes brought about by economic globalization. A key consequence of globalization, as mentioned above, was the strengthening of capital and the deregulation of the bargaining power of workers (Yeates 2001). In the era of the internationalized economy, its dominance over the weakened state due to globalization is observable (Mishra 1999). Businesses, therefore, have an increased influence both in the field of economics and in decision-making, which they can shape. In fact, their influence is increased through their participation in similar processes within the social dialogue, but also through the key positions that their executives receive in public bodies and organizations (Korpi 2006).

Strengthening the power of businesses in the new framework of strengthening market freedom and the shrinkage of the state has meant that they are more able to influence social policy-making. The empowerment of business power goes hand-in-hand with a broader framework for accelerating the economy vis-à-vis democracy (Crouch 2004). The imposition of market dictates leads to the undermining of democratic processes, as noted in Chap. 3.

In such a context, according to this approach, ways should be sought to find social policy measures that benefit business. This argument is reinforced by the fact that the economy is the state's main source of funding through the tax system. Therefore, if the economy deteriorates, then the state will suffer a fall in its revenues (Lalioti 2018).

References

Alcock, P., Erskine, A., & May, M. (Eds.). (1997). *The Student's Companion to Social Policy*. Oxford: Blackwell Publishers.

Barnes, C., & Mercer, G. (2003). *Disability*. Cambridge: Polity Press.

Bernaciak, M. (2012). Social Dumping: Political Catchphrase or Threat to Labour Standards? *ETUI Working Paper 2012.06*. Retrieved from SSRN: https://ssrn.com/abstract=2208393.

Beynon, H., & Nichols, T. (Eds.). (2006). *The Fordism of Ford and Modern Management: Fordism and Post-Fordism*. Cheltenham: Elgar.

Blackburn, R. (2008). What is Social Inequality? *International Journal of Sociology & Social Policy, 28*(7/8), 250–259.
Bonoli, G. (2013). *Origins of Active Social Policy: Labour Market and Childcare Policies in a Comparative Perspective*. Oxford: Oxford University Press.
Brubaker, R. (1992). *Citizenship and Nationhood in France and Germany*. Harvard University Press.
Byrne, D. (2005). *Social Exclusion*. London: Open University Press.
Carnoy, M., Castells, M., Cohen, S., & Fernando-Henrique, C. (Eds.). (1993). *The New Global Economy in the Information Age: Reflections on Our Changing World*. Pennsylvania: Pennsylvania University Press.
Copeland, P., & Papadimitriou, D. (Eds.). (2012). *The EU's Lisbon Strategy: Evaluating Success, Understanding Failure*. Basingstoke: Palgrave Macmillan.
Crouch, C. (2004). *Post-Democracy*. Indianapolis: Wiley.
Dean, H. (Ed.). (2004). *The Ethics of Welfare: Human Rights, Dependency, and Responsibility*. Bristol: Policy Press.
Dobson, A. (2000). Ecological Citizenship: A Disruptive Influence? In C. Pierson & S. Tormey (Eds.), *Politics at the Edge*. Basingstoke: Macmillan.
Dwyer, P. (2002). Making Sense of Social Citizenship: Some User Views on Welfare Rights and Responsibilities. *Critical Social Policy, 22*(2), 273–299.
Dwyer, P. (2004). *Understanding Social Citizenship*. Bristol: Policy Press.
Esping-Andersen, G. (1990). *The Three Worlds of Welfare Capitalism*. Cambridge: Polity Press.
Esping-Andersen, G. (1999). *Social Foundations of Postindustrial Economies*. Oxford: Oxford University Press.
Farnsworth, K., & Irving, Z. (Eds.). (2011). *Social Policy in Challenging Times. Economic Crisis and Welfare Systems*. Bristol: Policy Press.
Feronas, A. (2013). *The Europeanization of Social Policy. Theoretical Framework, Methodological Issues and the Greek Experience*. Athens: Dionicos (in Greek).
Ferrera, M., & Hemerijck, A. (2003). Recalibrating Europe's Welfare Regimes. In J. Zeitlin & D. M. Trubeck (Eds.), *Governing Work and Welfare in a New Economy: European and American Experiments*. Oxford: Oxford University Press.
Ferrera, M., & Rhodes, M. (2000). Recasting European Welfare States: An Introduction. *West European Politics, 23*(2), 1–10.
Fraser, N. (1995). From Redistribution to Recognition? Dilemmas of Justice in a 'Post-Socialist' Age. *New Left Review, 1*, 68–92.
Fraser, N. (2000). Rethinking Recognition. *New Left Review, 3*, 107–120.
Frericks, P. (2011). Marketising Social Protection in Europe: Two Distinct Paths and Their Impact on Social Inequalities. *International Journal of Sociology and Social Policy, 33*(5/6), 319–334.
Gaynor, N. (2011). In-Active Citizenship and the Depoliticization of Community Development in Ireland. *Community Development Journal, 46*(1), 27–41.

'he Death of the Social? Re-figuring the Territory of Government. *ociety, 25*(3), 327–356.
. *Women's Employment in Europe*. London: Routledge.
., & Berghman, J. (Eds.). (2004). *Connecting Welfare Diversity ropean Social Model*. Oxford: Intersentia.
). The European Social Model: Coping with the Challenges of *nal of Common Market Studies, 40*(4), 645–670.
Goodin, R. (1998). *Social Welfare and Individual Responsibility*. mbridge University Press.
The Politics of Welfare State Retrenchment: A Literature Review. *ad Administration, 40*(1), 104–120.
2). *Capitalists against Markets: The Making of Labour Markets States in the United States and Sweden*. Oxford: Oxford ss.
(1994). Postmodernism and Social Policy: A Great Leap *urnal of Social Policy, 23*(3), 385–404.
(2004). The Impact of New Social Risks on Welfare States. In by (Ed.), *New Risks, New Welfare: The Transformation of the are State*. Oxford: Oxford University Press.
10). *Inventing the Alternative. 'Identities' and 'Diversities' in the zation*. Athens: Kastanioti (in Greek).
1). The Erosion of Citizenship. *British Journal of Sociology,* 9.
13). *European Social Policy and Social Rights: The End of the* ed.). Athens: Topos (in Greek).
5). *Social Policy. Concepts and Relations* (p. 303). Athens: Topos
Tonkens, E. (2013). Talking Active Citizenship: Framing Welfare in England and the Netherlands. *Social Policy and Society,* 6.
Gender, Work, and Post-Fordism: The EC Context. *International ology, 24*(4), 67–82.
ton, G., & McDonald, C. (2011). The Role of Non-Profit in the Mixed Economy of Welfare-to-Work in the UK and *al Policy and Administration, 45*(3), 299–318.
. *Globalization and Social Policy*. London: Sage Publications.

George, V., & Wilding, P. (1994). *Welfare and Ideology*. London: Prentice Hall and Harvester Wheatsheaf.
Geyer, R. (2013). *Exploring European Social Policy*. Oxford: Wiley.
Giddens, A. (1998). *The Third Way: The Renewal of Social Democracy*. Cambridge: Polity Press.
Gilbert, N. (2002). *Transformation of the Welfare State: The Silent Surrender of Public Responsibility*. Oxford: Oxford University Press.
Gilbert, N. (2012). Citizenship in the Enabling State: The Changing Balance of Rights and Obilgations. In A. Evers & A. M. Guillemard (Eds.), *Social Policy and Citizenship: The Changing Landscape*. Oxford: Oxford University Press.
Gilbert, N., Burrows, R., & Pollert, A. (1992). *Fordism and Flexibility: Divisions and Change*. New York: St. Martin's Press.
Gough, I. (1980). Thatcherism and the Welfare State: Britain is Experiencing the Most Far-reaching Experiment in 'New Right' Politics in the Western World. *Marxism Today*. Reprinted in LSE Research Online: http://eprints.lse.ac.uk/66525/1/Binder1.pdf
Gravaris, D. (2018). Two Historical Forms of the Welfare State. In T. Sakellaropoulos, C. Economou, C. Skamnakis, & M. Angelaki (Eds.), *Social Policy*. Athens: Dionicos (in Greek).
Green, D. (1997). The Neo-Liberal Perspective. In P. Alcock, A. Erskine, & M. May (Eds.), *The Student's Companion to Social Policy*. Oxford: Blackwell.
Greenberg, E. (1981). Industrial Democracy and the Democratic Citizen. *The Journal of Politics, 43*(3), 964–981.
Habermas, J. (1994). Citizenship and National Identity. In B. V. Steenbergen (Ed.), *The Condition of Citizenship*. London: Sage Publications.
Hacker, J., & Pierson, P. (2002). Business Power and Social Policy: Employment and the Formation of the American Welfare State. *Politics and Society, 30*(2), 277–325.
Hall, P., & Soskice, D. (Eds.). (2001). *Varieties of Capitalism: The Institutional Foundations of Comparative Advantage*. Oxford: Oxford University Press.
Harvey, D. (2008). *The Condition of Postmodernity*. Cambridge: Wiley-Blackwell.
Heywood, A. (2005). *Political Ideologies*. London: Palgrave Macmillan.
Iversen, T., & Wren, A. (1998). Equality, Employment and Budgetary Restraint: The Trilemma of the Service Economy. *World Politics, 50*(4), 507–546.
Jackson, W. A. (1998). *The Political Economy of Population Ageing*. London and New York: Edward Elgar.
Jensen, P. H., & Pfau-Effinger, B. (2005). Active Citizenship: The New Face of Welfare. In J. G. Andersen, A. M. Guillemard, P. H. Jensen, & B. Pfau-Effinger (Eds.), *The Changing Face of Welfare*. London: Policy Press.
Jessop, B. (1993). Towards a Schumpeterian Workfare State? Preliminary Remarks on Post-Fordist Political Economy. *Studies in Political Economy, 40*(1), 7–39.

Johanssen, H., & Hvinden, B. (2013). Towards a Post-Marshallian Framework for the Analysis of Social Citizenship. In A. Evers & A. M. Guillemard (Eds.), *Social Policy and Citizenship: The Changing Landscape*. Oxford, UK: Oxford University Press.

Johnson, N. (Ed.). (2014). *Mixed Economies of Welfare: A Comparative Perspective*. London: Routledge.

Korpi, W. (2006). Power Resources and Employer-Centered Approaches in Explanations of Welfare States and Varieties of Capitalism: Protagonists, Consenters, and Antagonists. *World Politics, 58*(2), 167–206.

Kotsonopoulos, L. (2016). *The Lost Consensus. Welfare State, Capitalism and Democracy*. Athens: Sakis Karagiorgas Foundation (in Greek).

Kröger, S. (2009). The Open Method of Coordination: Underconceptualisation, Overdetermination, Depoliticisation and Beyond. *European Integration online Papers, 1*(13), 1–22.

Kvist, J., & Saari, J. (Eds.). (2007). *The Europeanisation of Social Protection*. Bristol: The Policy Press.

Lalioti, V. (2018). Theories of the Welfare State. In T. Sakellaropoulos, C. Economou, C. Skamnakis, & M. Angelaki (Eds.), *Social Policy*. Athens: Dionicos (in Greek).

Lemert, C. (2016). *Globalization*. London: Taylor & Francis.

Levitas, R. (1996). The Concept of Social Exclusion and the New Durkheimian Hegemony. *Critical Social Policy, 16*(2), 5–20.

Lister, R. (1998). *Citizenship: Feminist Perspectives*. Basingstoke: Macmillan.

Lowi, T. J. (1972). Four Systems of Policy, Politics, and Choice. *Public Administration Review, 32*(4), 298–310.

March, J., & Olsen, J. (1984). The New Institutionalism. Organizational Factors in Political Life. *American Political Science Review, 78*, 734–749.

Marinetto, M. (2003). Who Wants to Be an Active Citizen? The Politics and Practices of Community Involvement. *Sociology, 37*(1), 103–120.

Marshall, T. H. (1965). The Right to Welfare. *The Sociological Review, 13*(3), 261–272.

Mayer, V. (2008). Crafting a New Conservative Consensus on Welfare Reform: Redefining Citizenship, Social Provision, and the Public/Private Divide. *Social Politics, 15*(2), 154–181.

Mead, L. M. (Ed.). (1986). *Beyond Entitlement: The Social Obligations of Citizenship*. New York: Free Press.

Milligan, C., & Fyfe, N. (2005). Preserving Space for Volunteers: Exploring the Links between Voluntary Welfare Organisations, Volunteering and Citizenship. *Urban Studies, 42*(3), 417–433.

Mishra, R. (1999). *Globalization and the Welfare State*. Cheltenham: Edward Elgar.

Modood, T. (1992). *Not Easy Being British: Colour, Culture and Citizenship*. London: R.T. Trentham.

Murray, C. (1984). *Losing Ground: Am* Basic Books.

Murray, C. (1999). *The Underclass* Enterprise Institute.

Myles, J., & Quadagno, J. (2002). Pc *Service Review, 76*(1), 34–57.

Natali, D. (2010). The Lisbon Strateg *European Social Observatory No. 4.*

Navarro, V. (1998). Neoliberalism, 'G and the Welfare State. *Internati Administration, Evaluation, 28*(4)

Newman, J., & Tonkens, E. (Eds.) *Choice: Summoning the Active C* Amsterdam: Amsterdam Universit

O'Connor, J. (2002). Understandi Theoretical Perspectives. In D. *Perspectives*. Oxford University Pre

Pateman, C. (2000). The Patriarcha (Eds.), *The Welfare State: A Read*

Peters, G. (2019). *Institutional Institutionalism* (4th ed.). Chelte

Pfau-Effinger, B. (2004). *Culture,* Aldershot: Ashgate.

Pierson, C. (1991). *Beyond the Welfa* Cambridge: Polity Press.

Pierson, P. (1994). *Dismantling th Politics of Retrenchment*. Cambric

Pierson, P. (Ed.). (2001). *The New* University Press.

Powell, W., & Dimaggio, P. (Ed *Organizational Analysis*. Chicag

Preece, D. (2009). *Dismantling S Policy in the European Union*. Bc

Procacci, G. (2001). Poor Citizens: Welfare. In C. Crouch, K. Eder, & *the State*. Oxford: Oxford Unive

Putnam, R. (1993). What Makes *82*(2), 101–107.

Ramos, C. (2003). *Globalization a*

Rogne, L., Estes, C., Grossman, B *Social Insurance and Social Justi against Entitlements*. New York:

Rose, N. (*Econon*

Rubery, J.

Sakellarop *within*

Scharpf, F. Diversit

Schmidtz, Cambri

Starke, P. (*Social P*

Swenson, P *and We* Universi

Taylor-Goo Backwar

Taylor-Goo P. Taylor *Europea*

Tsoukalas, C *Age of Gl*

Turner, B. *52*(2), 18

Venieris, D. *Rapsody* (

Venieris, D. ((in Greek

Verhoeven, I. State Ref *12*(3), 41

Walby, S. (19 *Journal of*

Wright, S., M Organizati Australia.

Yeates, N. (20

CHAPTER 5

Responsible Citizenship and the Residualized Welfare State

5.1 The Responsible Citizenship Approach

The repercussions of the Great Recession of 2008 did not have a subversive effect on the directions in which the concept of citizenship was already travelling. On the contrary, they legitimized and accelerated the pre-crisis trend for weakening it. The individualized methodological reading of citizenship has intensified the tendency to override rights in favor of obligations and, in fact, with more abrupt changes (Verhoeven and Tonkens 2013). The economic crisis has been used more broadly as a vehicle for social policy restructuring. Consequently, responsible citizenship,[1] which forms the theoretical basis of the residualized welfare state, utilizes many concepts and tools that had been prepared even before the financial crisis.

The modern dominant discourse around citizenship has numerous dimensions, all of which center on the axis of individual responsibility. According to Lister (2011), the key components of responsible citizenship[2] are four: the agreement for a new welfare contract; prospects and

[1] Elsewhere it has been described as economic citizenship (see Kourachanis 2019).

[2] An alternative version with many similar features to Lister's was published before the crisis by John Clarke (2005). Clarke, examining New Labour's positions on citizenship, noted that it consists of four elements: activating; empowering; responsive or "responsibilized" citizenship; and abandonment of the "passive" benefits of the Keynesian model that were attached to postwar social citizenship.

N. Kourachanis, *Citizenship and Social Policy*,
https://doi.org/10.1007/978-3-030-59827-3_5

aspirations; consumerization; and, finally, the dimension of active citizenship. These four elements are summarized below.

The new welfare contract is the contract of the responsible society, and its main emphasis is on individual responsibility. The spirit of the new social contract is reflected in James Cameron's phrase, "'if you fail to take responsibility, then the free ride is over." As part of their responsibility, citizens must transfer as many of their social needs to the voluntary and private sectors as possible, so as not to burden public services.

The second dimension involves the perspectives and aspirations of citizens. This perspective points out that the concept of equality in the new welfare contract is replaced by the wording of the need for individuals to be competitive in the labor market. Responsible citizens should have ambitions such as improving their position through their own efforts and not with the help of the state (Lister 2011).

The next constituent of responsible citizenship is that of consumption. The legal basis of citizenship is replaced by an economic or consumer version of citizenship (Clarke et al. 2007). This means that every citizen can exercise his or her rights, as long as they are able to comply with market rules. The ideal citizen is, therefore, the one who can provide for their own social security, health protection and, in general, the promotion their well-being (Lynch et al. 2018). And, indeed, make the right consumer choices for themselves (Clarke 2005).

Finally, the theme of active citizenship relates to responsibilities for individual choices and responsibilities towards others. These responsibilities are more about making the right decisions for citizens, being more actively involved in the public sphere, and developing self-organizing or voluntary social support initiatives for those in need (Hviden and Takle 2017: 12). In this sense, the dominant rationale primarily focuses on how to activate the citizen to make social contributions.

In the midst of all these developments that result in the erosion of citizenship, some scholars, such as Turner (2016), pointed to a new version of it: *Denizenship*. Denizenship has started to emerge in the scholarly literature precisely because of the diminishing impact of citizenship in ensuring full participation in the political community. The denizen (from citizen) is a person who has the right to legal residence in a geographical area but has limited rights to welfare or political participation. The notion that Turner introduces into the scholarly literature divides it into two subcategories. The first version of the denizen (Denizen Type 1) is condensed into the above description and is intended primarily for economic migrants or refugees.

Murray, C. (1984). *Losing Ground: American Social Policy, 1950–1980*. New York: Basic Books.

Murray, C. (1999). *The Underclass Revisited*. Washington, DC: American Enterprise Institute.

Myles, J., & Quadagno, J. (2002). Political Theories of the Welfare State. *Social Service Review, 76*(1), 34–57.

Natali, D. (2010). The Lisbon Strategy, Europe 2020 and the Crisis in Between. *European Social Observatory No. 4*. Brussels.

Navarro, V. (1998). Neoliberalism, 'Globalization', Unemployment, Inequalities, and the Welfare State. *International Journal of Health Services: Planning, Administration, Evaluation, 28*(4), 607–682.

Newman, J., & Tonkens, E. (Eds.). (2011). *Participation, Responsibility and Choice: Summoning the Active Citizen in Western European Welfare States*. Amsterdam: Amsterdam University Press.

O'Connor, J. (2002). Understanding the Welfare State and Welfare States: Theoretical Perspectives. In D. Baer (Ed.), *Political Sociology: Canadian Perspectives*. Oxford University Press.

Pateman, C. (2000). The Patriarchal Welfare State. In C. Pierson & F. Castles (Eds.), *The Welfare State: A Reader*. Cambridge: Polity Press.

Peters, G. (2019). *Institutional Theory and Political Science. The New Institutionalism* (4th ed.). Cheltenham and Northampton: Edward Elgar.

Pfau-Effinger, B. (2004). *Culture, Welfare State and Women's Work in Europe*. Aldershot: Ashgate.

Pierson, C. (1991). *Beyond the Welfare State?: The new Political Economy of Welfare*. Cambridge: Polity Press.

Pierson, P. (1994). *Dismantling the Welfare State? Reagan, Thatcher, and the Politics of Retrenchment*. Cambridge: Cambridge University Press.

Pierson, P. (Ed.). (2001). *The New Politics of the Welfare State*. Oxford: Oxford University Press.

Powell, W., & Dimaggio, P. (Eds.). (1991). *The New Institutionalism in Organizational Analysis*. Chicago: University of Chicago Press.

Preece, D. (2009). *Dismantling Social Europe: The Political Economy of Social Policy in the European Union*. Boulder, CO: First Forum Press.

Procacci, G. (2001). Poor Citizens: Social Citizenship Versus Individualization of Welfare. In C. Crouch, K. Eder, & D. Tambini (Eds.), *Citizenship, Markets and the State*. Oxford: Oxford University Press.

Putnam, R. (1993). What Makes Democracy Work? *National Civic Review, 82*(2), 101–107.

Ramos, C. (2003). *Globalization and Technology*. Manila: Rex Book Store.

Rogne, L., Estes, C., Grossman, B., Hollister, B., & Solway, E. (Eds.). (2009). *Social Insurance and Social Justice: Social Security, Medicare and the Campaign against Entitlements*. New York: Springer.

Rose, N. (1996). The Death of the Social? Re-figuring the Territory of Government. *Economy and Society, 25*(3), 327–356.
Rubery, J. (1999). *Women's Employment in Europe*. London: Routledge.
Sakellaropoulos, T., & Berghman, J. (Eds.). (2004). *Connecting Welfare Diversity within the European Social Model*. Oxford: Intersentia.
Scharpf, F. (2002). The European Social Model: Coping with the Challenges of Diversity. *Journal of Common Market Studies, 40*(4), 645–670.
Schmidtz, D., & Goodin, R. (1998). *Social Welfare and Individual Responsibility*. Cambridge: Cambridge University Press.
Starke, P. (2006). The Politics of Welfare State Retrenchment: A Literature Review. *Social Policy and Administration, 40*(1), 104–120.
Swenson, P. (2002). *Capitalists against Markets: The Making of Labour Markets and Welfare States in the United States and Sweden*. Oxford: Oxford University Press.
Taylor-Gooby, P. (1994). Postmodernism and Social Policy: A Great Leap Backwards? *Journal of Social Policy, 23*(3), 385–404.
Taylor-Gooby, P. (2004). The Impact of New Social Risks on Welfare States. In P. Taylor-Gooby (Ed.), *New Risks, New Welfare: The Transformation of the European Welfare State*. Oxford: Oxford University Press.
Tsoukalas, C. (2010). *Inventing the Alternative. 'Identities' and 'Diversities' in the Age of Globalization*. Athens: Kastanioti (in Greek).
Turner, B. (2001). The Erosion of Citizenship. *British Journal of Sociology, 52*(2), 189–209.
Venieris, D. (2013). *European Social Policy and Social Rights: The End of the Rapsody* (2nd ed.). Athens: Topos (in Greek).
Venieris, D. (2015). *Social Policy. Concepts and Relations* (p. 303). Athens: Topos (in Greek).
Verhoeven, I., & Tonkens, E. (2013). Talking Active Citizenship: Framing Welfare State Reform in England and the Netherlands. *Social Policy and Society, 12*(3), 415–426.
Walby, S. (1994). Gender, Work, and Post-Fordism: The EC Context. *International Journal of Sociology, 24*(4), 67–82.
Wright, S., Marston, G., & McDonald, C. (2011). The Role of Non-Profit Organizations in the Mixed Economy of Welfare-to-Work in the UK and Australia. *Social Policy and Administration, 45*(3), 299–318.
Yeates, N. (2001). *Globalization and Social Policy*. London: Sage Publications.

Johanssen, H., & Hvinden, B. (2013). Towards a Post-Marshallian Framework for the Analysis of Social Citizenship. In A. Evers & A. M. Guillemard (Eds.), *Social Policy and Citizenship: The Changing Landscape*. Oxford, UK: Oxford University Press.

Johnson, N. (Ed.). (2014). *Mixed Economies of Welfare: A Comparative Perspective*. London: Routledge.

Korpi, W. (2006). Power Resources and Employer-Centered Approaches in Explanations of Welfare States and Varieties of Capitalism: Protagonists, Consenters, and Antagonists. *World Politics, 58*(2), 167–206.

Kotsonopoulos, L. (2016). *The Lost Consensus. Welfare State, Capitalism and Democracy*. Athens: Sakis Karagiorgas Foundation (in Greek).

Kröger, S. (2009). The Open Method of Coordination: Underconceptualisation, Overdetermination, Depoliticisation and Beyond. *European Integration online Papers, 1*(13), 1–22.

Kvist, J., & Saari, J. (Eds.). (2007). *The Europeanisation of Social Protection*. Bristol: The Policy Press.

Lalioti, V. (2018). Theories of the Welfare State. In T. Sakellaropoulos, C. Economou, C. Skamnakis, & M. Angelaki (Eds.), *Social Policy*. Athens: Dionicos (in Greek).

Lemert, C. (2016). *Globalization*. London: Taylor & Francis.

Levitas, R. (1996). The Concept of Social Exclusion and the New Durkheimian Hegemony. *Critical Social Policy, 16*(2), 5–20.

Lister, R. (1998). *Citizenship: Feminist Perspectives*. Basingstoke: Macmillan.

Lowi, T. J. (1972). Four Systems of Policy, Politics, and Choice. *Public Administration Review, 32*(4), 298–310.

March, J., & Olsen, J. (1984). The New Institutionalism. Organizational Factors in Political Life. *American Political Science Review, 78*, 734–749.

Marinetto, M. (2003). Who Wants to Be an Active Citizen? The Politics and Practices of Community Involvement. *Sociology, 37*(1), 103–120.

Marshall, T. H. (1965). The Right to Welfare. *The Sociological Review, 13*(3), 261–272.

Mayer, V. (2008). Crafting a New Conservative Consensus on Welfare Reform: Redefining Citizenship, Social Provision, and the Public/Private Divide. *Social Politics, 15*(2), 154–181.

Mead, L. M. (Ed.). (1986). *Beyond Entitlement: The Social Obligations of Citizenship*. New York: Free Press.

Milligan, C., & Fyfe, N. (2005). Preserving Space for Volunteers: Exploring the Links between Voluntary Welfare Organisations, Volunteering and Citizenship. *Urban Studies, 42*(3), 417–433.

Mishra, R. (1999). *Globalization and the Welfare State*. Cheltenham: Edward Elgar.

Modood, T. (1992). *Not Easy Being British: Colour, Culture and Citizenship*. London: R.T. Trentham.

George, V., & Wilding, P. (1994). *Welfare and Ideology*. London: Prentice Hall and Harvester Wheatsheaf.
Geyer, R. (2013). *Exploring European Social Policy*. Oxford: Wiley.
Giddens, A. (1998). *The Third Way: The Renewal of Social Democracy*. Cambridge: Polity Press.
Gilbert, N. (2002). *Transformation of the Welfare State: The Silent Surrender of Public Responsibility*. Oxford: Oxford University Press.
Gilbert, N. (2012). Citizenship in the Enabling State: The Changing Balance of Rights and Obilgations. In A. Evers & A. M. Guillemard (Eds.), *Social Policy and Citizenship: The Changing Landscape*. Oxford: Oxford University Press.
Gilbert, N., Burrows, R., & Pollert, A. (1992). *Fordism and Flexibility: Divisions and Change*. New York: St. Martin's Press.
Gough, I. (1980). Thatcherism and the Welfare State: Britain is Experiencing the Most Far-reaching Experiment in 'New Right' Politics in the Western World. *Marxism Today*. Reprinted in LSE Research Online: http://eprints.lse.ac.uk/66525/1/Binder1.pdf
Gravaris, D. (2018). Two Historical Forms of the Welfare State. In T. Sakellaropoulos, C. Economou, C. Skamnakis, & M. Angelaki (Eds.), *Social Policy*. Athens: Dionicos (in Greek).
Green, D. (1997). The Neo-Liberal Perspective. In P. Alcock, A. Erskine, & M. May (Eds.), *The Student's Companion to Social Policy*. Oxford: Blackwell.
Greenberg, E. (1981). Industrial Democracy and the Democratic Citizen. *The Journal of Politics, 43*(3), 964–981.
Habermas, J. (1994). Citizenship and National Identity. In B. V. Steenbergen (Ed.), *The Condition of Citizenship*. London: Sage Publications.
Hacker, J., & Pierson, P. (2002). Business Power and Social Policy: Employment and the Formation of the American Welfare State. *Politics and Society, 30*(2), 277–325.
Hall, P., & Soskice, D. (Eds.). (2001). *Varieties of Capitalism: The Institutional Foundations of Comparative Advantage*. Oxford: Oxford University Press.
Harvey, D. (2008). *The Condition of Postmodernity*. Cambridge: Wiley-Blackwell.
Heywood, A. (2005). *Political Ideologies*. London: Palgrave Macmillan.
Iversen, T., & Wren, A. (1998). Equality, Employment and Budgetary Restraint: The Trilemma of the Service Economy. *World Politics, 50*(4), 507–546.
Jackson, W. A. (1998). *The Political Economy of Population Ageing*. London and New York: Edward Elgar.
Jensen, P. H., & Pfau-Effinger, B. (2005). Active Citizenship: The New Face of Welfare. In J. G. Andersen, A. M. Guillemard, P. H. Jensen, & B. Pfau-Effinger (Eds.), *The Changing Face of Welfare*. London: Policy Press.
Jessop, B. (1993). Towards a Schumpeterian Workfare State? Preliminary Remarks on Post-Fordist Political Economy. *Studies in Political Economy, 40*(1), 7–39.

A second version of the denizen (Denizen Type 2) relates to the effects of the erosion of postwar social citizenship. The weakening of the influence of T. H. Marshall's approach in constructing the conditions for full citizen participation in modern Western societies shapes a form of citizenship the strong features of which are its temporary, insecure and limited ability to participate in the political community. Reducing equal opportunities for social participation drives modern citizens, especially those in need of social rights, into a finer, fragmented, and fragile social bond with the public sphere (Turner 2016). As a result, Denizen Type 1 and Denizen Type 2 are in a process of convergence that results in the erosion of citizenship.

Beyond these arguments, the notions of social investment and social innovation play a central role in the theoretical construction of citizenship at the beginning of the twenty-first century. All the new conceptual tools of social policy focus entirely on an individual empowerment approach. The activation policy goes hand-in-hand with a set of individual training measures (Esping-Andersen et al. 2002). However, such a logic does not go together with the existence of a safety net that ensures decent living. On the contrary, any social support action is inspired by the philosophy of helping individuals acquire certain skills. Individual independence and guidance for self-action, prudence, responsibility and entrepreneurship are fundamental components of the new interventionist spirit (Woolford and Nelund 2013), promoted through the concepts of social investment and social innovation.

More specifically, the concept of social investment in social policy was combined with Giddens' (1998) view of the state of social investment. According to Giddens, this form of state intervention is closely intertwined with the Third Way approach. It is an invention that proposes the transformation of the state into an entrepreneur. Expenditure takes the form of investing in human capital by shaping a citizen capable of facing the risks associated with that status. According to Giddens, leading social investment strategies are the development of lifelong learning and an emphasis on the social economy. However, these are actions whose benefits will be evident over the long term rather than directly, as is the case with income redistribution policies (Jenson and Saint-Martin 2003).

The social investment perspective, therefore, departs from the principle of income redistribution policies and converges with a perspective based on the strengthening of the individual skills and economic competitiveness of citizens. Child poverty is a popular area of application for social investment policies, as such policies are considered to act as a preventive for future empowerment (Esping-Andersen et al. 2002). By these means, citizens can cope with the risks and changes resulting from structural changes in the market (Sherraden 2003). This interventionist philosophy confirms the primacy of the market, while the state is primarily concerned with making it easier for citizens to cope with the risks concealed by the market (Petmesidou 2014).

The recent concept of social innovation refers to new, "smart" ways of addressing social needs. The shift in and use of the term "innovation", from the economic to the social field, corresponds with the gamut of changes being made by the entrepreneurial state. "Social innovation" means locally embedded practices and policies that can lead to satisfying the social needs of those affected by poverty and social exclusion and who do not find adequate responses to these needs from the state's social policies or the private market (European Commission 2013b: 15).

Social innovations are processes by which civil society actors develop new technologies, strategies and ideas or organizations to meet social needs or to solve social problems (Cajaiba-Santana 2014). The role of the active citizen and local authorities is therefore crucial to this approach. The combination of these two players is believed to be able to bring about faster, more effective needs for identification, targeted solutions and immediate responses in resolving social issues (Keller Lauritzen 2013: 5).

As will be explained in Sect. 5.3 on the legitimacy of the residualized welfare state in the wake of the crisis, the concepts of social investment and social innovation have been transformed into key elements of social policy action in the latest EU Strategy, the "Europe 2020 Strategy." The context and its content will be presented following a critique of the concept of responsible citizenship.

5.2 Critics of the Responsible Citizenship Approach

The foundation of responsible citizenship is a second, more intensive, phase of the strengthening of individual obligations and the weakening of citizens' social rights. The transition to responsible citizenship in the context of neoliberal globalization goes hand-in-hand with the cultivation of a more individualistic society. The basic value of this form of social organization is that each person seeks to serve their own interests (Moreno 2016). The dimension of accountability in citizenship is at the heart of the neoliberal political program (Joppke 2008; Muehlebach 2012).

In this version of responsible individualism, the fulfillment of multiple (mainly financial) obligations in order to exercise one's rights is a factor that erodes social citizenship (Dwyer 2004). The increasing number of eligibility criteria act as filters that exclude citizens from social rights (Ferrarini et al. 2013). As part of the effort to promote social policy reforms, these filters have been legitimized as a way to improve citizens' accountability.

In the most common version of responsible individualism, employment has been the most important condition for accessing social benefits both before (Levitas 1998) and during the crisis (Dwyer and Wright 2014; Edmiston 2017). During the crisis, eligibility criteria were expanded while, at the same time, the level of social benefits shrank, further eroding the impact of citizenship. The current texture of citizenship has elements more of social control, which undermines the sought-after emancipation that citizenship itself proclaims (Patrick 2017).

The social support provided by the social investment state is almost depleted for the purpose of enhancing citizens' individual skills, through the basic tools of education and active employment policies (Lister 2004). Indeed, this excessive regulation of responsible citizenship is inversely proportional to the widespread deregulation of the social protection system. At the same time, there is a residualized spectrum of protection for extreme poverty management, within which the presence of civil society and private social policy actors is particularly dynamic.

The crisis has also contributed to the consolidation of welfare pluralism as a central philosophy for resolving social problems. As Carmel and Papadopoulos (2009) rightly point out, these developments are of major political significance. They disconnect citizenship from the state and political processes by favoring the notion of referring citizens to a range of organizations in order for their needs to be met, although these are not, however, accountable for their actions. The effect of such practices is to encourage the depoliticization of citizens (Bruszt and Vedres 2008).

Undoubtedly, the view of the social investment state is in line with the neoliberal conception of the primacy of market mechanisms and the language of the individualization of social risks, with the exception that the state is responsible for creating the conditions through which people deal with them (Petmesidou 2014: 24). However, the austerity inherent in the social policies of this economy-centric version of citizenship undermines its effectiveness and universality (Edmiston 2017).

5.3 The Acceleration of the Residualization of the Welfare State

The Great Recession of 2008 caused a chain effect on a global scale. In order to manage it, the EU's central policy decisions opted for a reduction in budget spending (Bermeo and Pontusson 2012). It was, therefore, an economic downturn full of paradoxes. The most important of these was to reinforce, rather than reject, the dominant ideology that led to it (Papatheodorou 2014).

In light of the political choices discussed below, it will be argued that the Great Recession of 2008 was used as a vehicle to legitimize social policy restructuring. This is the second phase of leaving the welfare state behind, with rapid reforms and more abrupt deregulation policies where needed. Indeed, in order to serve this neoliberal plan, deviations from democratic principles have often been observed (Petmesidou 2014; Armingeon and Guthmann 2014; Hoffmann-Lange 2015). The procedures and methods used to enforce and implement the financial adjustment programs are outlined below.

In the wake of the crisis, the economy-centric nature of the EU has been reoriented in an ordoliberal direction (Dale and El-Enany 2013), pushing ahead with pre-existing economic policy. This was done through the 2011 "six-pack" that amended the Stability and Growth Pact, the 2012 Financial Pact and the "two-pack" of 2013 for evaluating draft national budgets. The proclaimed aim of this has been to avoid unsustainable public finances. Thus, the demand for balanced Member-State budgets, the triggering of emergency state mechanisms and widespread cuts in social spending have shaped the new socioeconomic landscape (Dimoulas and Kouzis 2018: 11).

All of these new governance tools help strengthen Member States' budgetary discipline by imposing stricter supervision and control rules (de la Porte and Heins 2015). However, this is yet another aspect of the asphyxiating economic harmonization policies which, contrary to the practices of voluntary social convergence, are further ingredients that have been added to a negative mix that aggravates social restructuring. This mix is also shaped by the escalation of social problems, due to at least three factors: the gradual crisis of social policy before the economic crisis, due to the pre-existing neoliberal direction that was being taken; the impact of the crisis on deteriorating social conditions; and the overwhelming poverty that austerity policies brought about through widespread cuts in social protection systems.

Another aspect of the new management mix imposed by the European institutions was the succession of policy shocks implemented through the fiscal adjustment programs for the economies of those Member States that had resorted to requesting international financial support (Mahon et al. 2015). Greece first, then Ireland, Portugal and Cyprus were forced to implement the financial requirements of the Institutions, with significant social implications. These policies came to be known in public discourse as the "memoranda" (or bailout programs). Their imposition resulted in an intrinsic contradiction: widespread weakening of social policy coinciding with a sharp rise in social problems (Kourachanis 2019).

The memoranda were designed in a highly technocratic manner (Hardiman et al. 2017: 4) and their adoption was intended to serve multiple purposes, including reducing fiscal deficits and achieving surpluses, ensuring the sustainability of public debt, rescuing and stabilizing the financial system, stimulating the competitiveness of national economies and restoring the ability to borrow from the international financial markets (European Commission 2010: 39–42). This approach served a one-dimensional technical rationale for meeting quantitative objectives. The seeds of this apolitical perception were already embodied in the reform programs of the 1990s implemented in the context of European integration (Preece 2009).

An unprecedented feature of the policy mix adopted for all four countries was the involvement of the International Monetary Fund (IMF), its first participation in an EU Member State support program. The IMF, together with the World Bank, are two key institutions for practicing global economic governance in a neoliberal manner (Guven 2012: 869). Some of the main general elements of its interventions were the intensive contraction in social policy spending, the deregulation of labor relations and wage cuts, and the extensive privatization of public property (Danaher 1994).

In this dire environment of recession, the "Europe 2020 Strategy" was called upon to shape the EU's key new directions in the midst of crisis. The three priorities set were smart growth, sustainable development and inclusive growth [COM (2010) 2020 final]. As regards inclusive growth, the aim was to achieve a high-employment economy that would attain social and territorial cohesion. From this very first formulation of the priorities of the last European strategy, it is clear that development remains the focal point around which all the issues under consideration revolve.

Among the primary objectives of Europe 2020, in social policy terms, were: to increase employment rates from 69 % to 75 % of the productive population; to reduce early school leaving rates from 15 % to 10 %; and to reduce the number of Europeans living below the national poverty line by 20 million. The European Platform for Poverty Reduction was introduced as a central flagship initiative in the field of social policy [COM (2010) 2020 final].

At the EU Community level this objective has been pursued through three sub-pillars: first, by transforming the Open Method of Coordination for social exclusion and social protection into a platform for co-operation, evaluation and exchange of best practices, as a means of combating poverty and poverty. Social exclusion and targeted aid to promote these actions will come from structural funds, such as the European Social Fund. Second, by designing and implementing programs to promote social innovation for the most vulnerable people, with a focus on developing innovative education, training and employment opportunities for vulnerable groups. And, third, by assessing the viability of social protection and retirement systems.

A key tool for the implementation of the strategy was the Social Investment Package, which was published in 2013 with the aim of contributing to the implementation of the strategy. The package provided guidance to Member States on developing more effective social policies to address the significant social challenges they faced as a result of the economic crisis and demographic changes.

The main purpose of the Social Investment Package was to focus on human skills. Policies were geared towards empowering human capacities and implementing support actions that created opportunities for full-time employment and social life. In this context, its objectives were directed toward a more efficient allocation of resources to ensure adequate and sustainable social protection systems, to invest in skills and competences, so that individuals were more likely to integrate into society and the labor market and, finally, toward more effective social protection systems that responded to the needs of individuals at critical times in their lives (European Commission 2013a).

At the same time, Europe 2020 dominate the concept of social innovation. As embodied in the philosophy of the Strategy, social innovation offered solutions to social demands and challenges. This is because they achieved greater effectiveness through partnerships between the public and private sectors, as well as with the active involvement of civil society.

At this point it is worth noting that the term "social innovation" has often been used for social policy issues in recent years. An important aspect of it is to find ways to reduce bureaucratic costs and increase the social efficiency of social services by shaping a framework for innovative ventures in the service sector. In this context, the development of flexibility and innovation practices are seen as cost-effective solutions for the formulation of social interventions.

The Platform for Combating Poverty and Social Exclusion promoted social experimentation in the fields of social policy. The fundamental principle of the concept of social experimentation is to pilot a social intervention on a small sample of the population in order to test its effectiveness, before deciding whether to apply it on a general scale (J-Pal Europe 2011: 2). Social innovations, in one approach, refer to locally integrated practices and policies that help those affected by poverty and social exclusion to meet their basic needs; needs for which they do not find satisfactory solutions in macro-level social policies or in the private market (Oosterlynck et al. 2013: 3). For the above reasons, the Platform for Innovation framework is implemented through partnerships between the state, civil society and the market, through broadening and enhancing stakeholder engagement but also through social economy and social entrepreneurship actions [COM (2010) 2020 Final].

Economic, political and social developments during the Great Recession of 2008 highlight the absolute legitimacy of market primacy over the welfare state. This is illustrated by the practices that were followed in order to consolidate the residual welfare state, which offered even greater scope for freedom in the private economy. Any resistance to the transfer of social policy responsibilities from the state to non-state actors had been stifled with the outbreak of the crisis (Fine 2012). The very imposition of ruthless neoliberalism as a one-way street led European welfare states to noticeable deregulation (Hermann 2017), which consequently exacerbated social problems.

The crisis offered the much sought-after reason to legitimize welfare pluralism as the dominant philosophy of social intervention. In the days of austerity, the establishment of NGOs as the breakthrough resolution to growing social problems gained social acceptance, as many states experienced fiscal bankruptcy. At such a juncture, civil society actors were called upon, at the non-governmental level, to replace state accountability and, at the social movement level, to highlight the significant decoupling of social rights from citizenship. The crisis itself was thus exploited by the dominant political forces as a vehicle for further minimizing state intervention in the social field (Stockhammer 2012).

In the context of the residualization of the welfare state, the recommodification of social benefits has accelerated. The legal basis of citizenship is replaced by a version of responsible citizenship that has the capacity to "consume" social benefits (Clarke et al. 2007). This means that every citizen can exercise their rights as long as they can fulfill their responsibilities under market rules. The responsible citizen/consumer, in this form of individualized and commercialized social protection, should be proactive so that at no point in their life will they experience social disadvantages that cannot be faced alone (Blackburn 2008: 256).

5.4 Interpretations of the Residualized Welfare State

The Great Recession of 2008 gave rise to accelerated procedures to legitimize the residualization of the welfare state, continuing a trend that had begun before the crisis in a mild and reformed way. One result of the abrupt and deregulatory interventions in social protection systems was attempts to interpret the transformation of these systems during the crisis and the economic downturn as an independent variable. This is central to the whole spectrum of specific interpretive ventures and a number of different approaches influenced by neo-institutionalism, fiscal sociology and interpretative approaches that focus on discourse have sought to explain why the crisis led to a version of the residualized welfare state.

A first attempt at interpreting the roots of the Great Recession of 2008 falls under the category of neo-institutional approaches that focus on the varieties of capitalism. Central to this matrix of analysis is the growth model adopted by institutions across the world, including Europe (Iversen et al. 2016). It also concerns its impact on the economies of the Member States. The rules established by the institutions have not provided for procedures to balance governments' current budget deficits. In addition, there are no institutional means to tackle global imbalances, with the result that the various models of capitalist development are reproduced in ways that cause recurring economic problems such as the 2008 Great Recession (Iversen and Soskice 2013). All these developments highlight the structural deficiencies of Economic and Monetary Union and the institutional capacity to manage a large-scale crisis. The over-indebtedness of the national economies plays an important role.

The economies of the countries of the periphery, such as Greece, Portugal, Spain and Cyprus, as well as Ireland, were unable to manage their national debt, leading to the imposition of stifling fiscal cuts by European institutions and the International Monetary Fund (McBride et al. 2015). The very process of crisis management itself through the logic of budget cuts and the depletion of social protection led to escalating inequalities between the developed economies of Northern and Western Europe and the countries of the Southeast (Johnston and Regan 2016).

Other studies of the origins of neo-institutionalism point to the Great Recession of 2008 as the culmination of the financial control procedures initiated by the Oil Crisis of the1970. These processes, under the influence of neoliberalism, took the form of state policies designed to weaken the employment protection framework and to reshuffle the balance of social forces in favor of the capitalist order (Heyes et al. 2012). The shrinking bargaining power of labor unions and their inability to influence the public policy agenda in the last quarter of the twentieth century have played an important role in the emergence of the current crisis (Nolan 2011).

A similar logic holds for the approach that Petmesidou (2014: 21–3) calls policy drift. The perspective of drift argues that the social role of public policy depends not only on the content of statutory laws but also on the dynamic way in which these laws interact with economic and social conditions. Thus, laws may remain unchanged but the redistributive scope of social policies can be limited by economic recession or austerity policies (Hacker 2004).

According to Pierson (2011), this inherent contradiction has been present in recent years. The resilience of social spending for certain actions coincides with the sharpening of social inequalities. These changes in social indicators do not derive so much from the range of new social risks as described above, but from political decisions for changes to the institutions governing labor relations, the taxation system, fiscal discipline, and more. Changes that exacerbate social inequalities, erode the redistributive effect of social protection institutions and adjust any directions taken to better serve the interests of the economic oligarchy.

For the above reasons, a main argument of the neo-institutionalism approach is that sustainable economic growth depends not only on sound financial choices, but also on the formation of appropriate institutional infrastructures that can provide safeguards to prevent fiscal slippage. To this end, it is necessary to adapt economic and social policies to the appropriate institutional conditions of each different type of political economy (Hall 2017).

A second category are the analyses that have the characteristics of fiscal sociology (see Kotsonopoulos 2016: 223–4). These analyses connect the crisis to the relationship that states have developed with global financial markets. In these interpretations, an invisible thread links the financial crisis of 2008 to the oil crisis of the 1970s. These are structural crises of the capitalist system.

According to these analyses, the recession of the 1970s resulted in welfare states making massive fiscal cuts. Other policies, such as the liberalization of the financial markets, led to an increase in private debt, as reflected in the 2008 crisis. In order to rescue the financial system, states undertook debt management, which resulted in fiscal deflection. In short, a process of socializing the costs of the financial system has been carried out, sacrificing a large part of social protection systems. In such an environment, the balance between capitalism and democracy seems to be reoriented towards a market democracy (Kotsonopoulos 2016: 223–6).

Wolff, in his book *Capitalism Hits the Fan* (2010), interprets the 2008 crisis as a consequence of the mix of post-1970 profit explosion, the expansion of the debt-laden financial system and the bubble of the real estate market, all of which resulted in the stagnation of wages. American workers were forced to resort to a malfunctioning borrowing and debt spiral that eventually burst through with the collapse of mortgage lending. By placing the 2008 crisis in this broader historical and systematic context, Wolff argues that the rescue programs, in the manner they were implemented and with their particular content, were not sufficient to address the real causes of the crisis.

Another study that addresses the issue of over-indebtedness is that of Lazzarato (2011). Lazzarato points out that financial debt is at the heart of the neoliberal program. It is a political conception that produces conditions of dependence between the creditor and the debtor. Debt is not a disadvantage of the dominant ideology; rather, it is the driving force behind the profitability of the upper social classes. The debt economy is a product of capitalism which serves to reduce the welfare state and to carry out an inverted redistribution at the expense of socially weaker groups and to the benefit of economic elites. At the same time, it acts as a mechanism for governing collective and individual bodies through the creditor–debtor relationship. The financial crisis of 2008 was a turning point in the complete transformation from the welfare state to the construction of the indebted person, something that has been sought for four decades by the power bloc. Thus, the austerity policies that the neoliberal political program consolidated focus on sharp cuts in social protection systems and public services in general (Lazzarato 2011).

Other researchers argue that the first crisis of the twenty-first century is the third crisis in economic theory. This is a crisis that affects both orthodox and heterodox approaches. This crisis follows the first one, which dates back to the 1980s, and the second of the 1990s. A new type of financial instability has emerged in the new capitalist morphology, and thus new processes appear in themselves unsustainable (Bellofiore and Halevi 2011).

Wolfgang Streeck's (2014) study argues that the 2008 crisis is part of a deep process of the restructuring of the postwar Keynesian capitalist model that began in the 1970s. As Western economic growth rates began to decline in the 1970s, the balance between financial profitability and electoral success became increasingly difficult. This is where the dilemma of the divergence between democracy and the financial system emerges. The Great Recession of 2008 brought precisely this conflict between the popular will and the markets into the open. It will end with the predominance of either capitalism or of democracy; for the time being, the former is prevailing over the latter. This restructuring has been described as a counter-revolution of capital against the postwar redistributive interventionism of the countries the West and the restoration of the primacy of the economy over democracy (Streeck 2014).

Finally, Kilman (2015) attributes the Great Recession to subjective causes. The rate of return on investment in US fixed assets declined throughout the fifty-year period before the recession. The slowdown in investment led to a slowdown in economic growth, which has been the main cause of rising public debt and the subsequent cuts (Kilman 2015).

The third interpretative approach focuses on the discourse constructed to legitimize the residualized tendency of the welfare state. This approach considers the broader context in which the public discourse on the legitimizing of deregulation takes place as well as to the pleasant-sounding developments that accompany it. Here, systemic media, government spokespeople and other public or informal actors influencing public opinion are recruited to promote cuts in social spending as necessary or as long-term interventions that serve the sustainability of the social protection system (Petmesidou 2014: 20).

A number of studies have addressed this interpretive dimension in the current crisis years. Vis (2009), using the behavioral theory of perspective, argues that it is necessary to shape the deteriorating socioeconomic situation in order to implement unpopular reforms. In particular, she argues that the extent to which a government undertakes unpopular reforms in any given period depends on the magnitude of the political costs.

If a government acts within comfortable socioeconomic conditions (e.g. a thriving economy, low unemployment) and/or a stable political position (e.g. a large parliamentary majority), it will avoid the risk of proceeding with anti-social reforms. Conversely, if the socioeconomic conditions are unfavorable (e.g. economic recession, high unemployment rates) and/or the government's position is politically weak (e.g. low polling rates), then it will accept the risk of making difficult political changes. Therefore, shaping a political risk situation is essential for undertaking bold reforms (Vis 2009). In a similar vein, Hollanders and Vis (2013) point out that governments only take anti-social measures during times of bad economic conditions. This is due to the fact that at times when social problems are being exacerbated, voters expect to see robust political change.

A typical example of the construction of a beautiful vocabulary that serves to legitimize political goals rather than reflect reality is the field of EU social policies. In both the Lisbon Strategy and the Europe 2020 Strategy, social policy objectives were extremely ambitious, although a corresponding level of social progress has not been made. On the contrary, particularly in the context of the crisis, social inequalities have worsened. Ambitious political rhetoric goes hand-in-hand with rigorous austerity measures (Petmesidou 2014: 39–41). In this sense, the case of EU social policies embodies the construction of a discourse that has no real content but instead seeks to mitigate the political costs of the residual social policies that are being practiced.

References

Armingeon, K., & Guthmann, K. (2014). Democracy in Crisis? The Declining Support for National Democracy in European Countries, 2007–2011. *European Journal of Political Research, 53*(3), 423–442.

Bellofiore, R., & Halevi, J. (2011). The Great Recession and the Third Crisis in Economic Theory. In E. Brancaccio & J. Fontana (Eds.), *The Global Economic Crisis. New Perspectives on the Critique of Economic Theory and Policy*. London and New York: Routledge.

Bermeo, N., & Pontusson, J. (Eds.). (2012). *Coping with Crisis. Government Reactions to the Great Recession*. New York: Russell Sage Foundation.

Blackburn, R. (2008). What is Social Inequality? *International Journal of Sociology & Social Policy, 28*(7/8), 250–259.

Bruszt, L., & Vedres, B. (2008). The Politics of Civic Combinations. *Voluntas, 19*(2), 140–160.

Cajaiba-Santana, G. (2014). Social Innovation: Moving the Field Forward. A Conceptual Framework. *Technological Forecasting and Social Change, 82*, 42–51.

Carmel, E., & Papadopoulos, T. (2009). Governing Social Security: From Protection to Markets. In J. Millar & R. Sainsbury (Eds.), *Understanding Social Security: Issues for Policy and Practice*. Bristol: Policy Press.

Clarke, J. (2005). New Labour's Citizens: Activated, Empowered, Responsibilized, Abandoned? *Critical Social Policy, 25*(4), 447–463.

Clarke, J., Newman, J., Smith, N., Vidler, E., & Westmarland, L. (2007). *Creating Citizen–Consumers: Changing Publics and Changing Public Services*. London: Sage.

Dale, G., & El-Enany, N. (2013). The Limits of Social Europe: EU Law and the Ordoliberal Agenda. *German Law Journal, 14*(5), 613–649.

Danaher, K. (Ed.). (1994). *Fifty Years is Enough: The Case against the World Bank and the International Monetary Fund*. Boston: South End Press.

de la Porte, C., & Heins, E. (Eds.). (2015). *The Sovereign Debt Crisis, the EU and Welfare State Reform*. Basingstoke: Palgrave Macmillan.

Dimoulas, C., & Kouzis, I. (2018). Introduction. In C. Dimoulas & I. Kouzis (Eds.), *Crisis and Social Policy in Greece. Deadlocks and Solutions*. Athens: Topos (in Greek).

Dwyer, P. (2004). Creeping Conditionality in the UK: From Welfare Rights to Conditional Entitlements? *The Canadian Journal of Sociology, 29*(2), 265–287.

Dwyer, P., & Wright, S. (2014). Universal Credit, Ubiquitous Conditionality and Its Implications for Social Citizenship. *Journal of Poverty and Social Justice, 22*(1), 27–35.

Edmiston, D. (2017). Welfare, Austerity and Social Citizenship in the UK. *Social Policy and Society, 16*(2). https://doi.org/10.1017/S1474746416000531.

Esping-Andersen, G., Gallie, D., Hemerijck, A., & Myles, J. (Eds.). (2002). *Why We Need a New Welfare State*. Oxford: Oxford University Press.

European Commission. (2010). European Economy. The Economic Adjustment Programme for Greece. *Occasional Papers 61*. Brussels.

European Commission. (2013a). Social Investment Package. Brussels.

European Commission. (2013b). Social Innovation Research in the European Union. Brussels.

Ferrarini, T., Nelson, K., & Höög, H. (2013). From Universalism to Selectivity: Old Wine in New Bottles for Child Benefits in Europe and Other Countries. In I. Marx & K. Nelson (Eds.), *Minimum Income Protection in Flux. Reconciling Work and Welfare in Europe*. London: Palgrave Macmillan.

Fine, B. (2012). Financialization and Social Policy. In P. Utting, S. Razavi, & R. Varghese Buchholz (Eds.), *The Global Crisis and Transformative Social Change*. London: Palgrave Macmillan.

Giddens, A. (1998). *The Third Way: The Renewal of Social Democracy*. Cambridge: Polity Press.

Guven, A. B. (2012). The IMF, the World Bank, and the Global Economic Crisis: Exploring Paradigm Continuity. *Development and Change, 43*(4), 869–898.

Hacker, J. (2004). Privatizing Risk without Privatizing the Welfare State: The Hidden Politics of Social Policy Retrenchment in the United States. *American Political Science Review, 98*(2), 243–260.

Hall, P. A. (2017). Varieties of Capitalism in Light of the Euro Crisis. *Journal of European Public Policy*. https://doi.org/10.1080/13501763.2017.1310278.

Hardiman, N., Araujo, J. F., MacCarthaigh, M., & Spanou, C. (2017). The Troika's Variations on a Trio: Why the Loan Programmes Worked so Differently in Greece, Ireland, and Portugal. *Discussion Paper*. Dublin: UCD.

Hermann, C. (2017). Crisis, Structural Reform and the Dismantling of the European Social Model(s). *Economic and Industrial Democracy, 38*(1), 51–68.

Heyes, J., Lewis, P., & Clark, I. (2012). Varieties of Capitalism, Neoliberalism and the Economic Crisis of 2008–? *Industrial Relations Journal, 43*(3), 222–241.

Hoffmann-Lange, U. (2015). The Impact of the Great Recession on Support for Democracy. *Taiwan Journal of Democracy, 11*(1), 53–78.

Hollanders, D., & Vis, D. (2013). Voters' Commitment Problem and Reforms in Welfare Programs. *Public Choice, 155*, 433–448.

Hviden, B., & Takle, M. (2017). Concept Paper for Activating Social Citizenship. *Report*. SOLIDUS Project, Deliverable 4.1, HORIZON 2020.

Iversen, T., & Soskice, D. (2013). *A Structural-Institutional Explanation of the Eurozone Crisis*. Paper presented at the Political Economy Workshop at the London School of Economics, June 3, 2013. Retrieved from http://www.people.fas.harvard.edu/~iversen/PDFfiles/Iversen&Soskice_euro2015.pdf

Iversen, T., Soskice, D., & Hope, A. (2016). The Eurozone and Political Economic Institutions. *Annual Review of Political Science, 19*, 163–185.

Jenson, J., & Saint-Martin, D. (2003). New Routes to Social Cohesion? Citizenship and the Social Investment State. *The Canadian Journal of Sociology, 28*(1), 77–99.

Johnston, A., & Regan, A. (2016). European Monetary Integration and the Incompatibility of National Varieties of Capitalism. *Journal of Common Market Studies, 54*(2), 318–336.

Joppke, C. (2008). Comparative Citizenship: A Restrict Turn in Europe. *Law and Ethics of Human Rights, 2*(1), 1–41.

J-Pal Europe. (2011). Social Experimentation: A Methodological Guide for Policy Makers. Directorate General for Employment, Social Affairs and Inclusion.

Keller Lauritzen, R. J. (2013). *Social Innovation in Local Government. Experiences from Denmark*. Danish Technological Institute.

Kilman, A. (2015). The Great Recession and Marx's Crisis Theory. *The American Journal of Economics and Sociology, 74*(2), 236–277.

Kotsonopoulos, L. (2016). *The Lost Consensus. Welfare State, Capitalism and Democracy*. Athens: Sakis Karagiorgas Foundation (in Greek).

Kourachanis, N. (2019). Homelessness Policies in the Liberal and the Southern European Welfare Regimes: Ireland, Portugal, and Greece. *Housing Policy Debate*. https://doi.org/10.1080/10511482.2019.1641733.

Lazzarato, M. (2011). *The Making of the Indebted Man an Essay on the Neoliberal Condition*. Los Angeles, CA: Semiotext(e).

Levitas, R. (1998). *The Inclusive Society? Social Exclusion and New Labour*. Basingstoke: Macmillan.

Lister, R. (2004). The Third Way's Social Investment State. In J. Lewis & R. Surender (Eds.), *Welfare State Change: Towards a Third Way?* Oxford: Oxford University Press.

Lister, R. (2011). The Age of Responsibility: Social Policy and Citizenship in the Early 21st Century. *Social Policy Review, 23*, 63–84.

Lynch, K., Kalaitzake, M., & Crean, M. (2018). Research Report on the Conceptualization of European Solidarity. Dublin: UCD.

Mahon, R., Boychuk, G. W., & McBride, S. (2015). Introduction. In S. McBride, R. Mahon, & G. Boychuk (Eds.), *After '08: Social Policy and the Global Financial Crisis*. Vancouver: UBC Press.

McBride, S., Mahon, R., & Boychuk, G. (Eds.). (2015). *After '08: Social Policy and the Global Financial Crisis*. Vancouver: UBC Press.

Moreno, L. (2016). Post-crisis and the Bronze Age of Welfare in Europe. *Working Paper*. Instituto de Políticas y Bienes Públicos (IPP) CSIC, Madrid.

Muehlebach, A. (2012). *The Moral Neoliberal: Welfare and Citizenship in Italy*. Chicago: University of Chicago Press.

Nolan, P. (2011). Money, Markets, Meltdown: The 21st-Century Crisis of Labour. *Industrial Relations Journal, 42*(1), 2–17.

Oosterlynck, S., Kazepov, Y., Novy, A., Cools, P., Barberis, E., Wukovitsch F., Sarius, T., & Leubolt, B. (2013). The Butterfly and the Elephant: Local Social Innovation, the Welfare State and New Poverty Dynamics. *IMPROVE Discussion Paper 13(03)*. Antwerp: Herman Deleeck Centre for Social Policy—University of Antwerp.

Papatheodorou, C. (2014). Economic Crisis, Poverty and Deprivation in Greece. The Impact of Neoliberal Remedies. In S. Mavroudeas (Ed.), *Greek Capitalism in Crisis: Marxist Analyses*. London: Routledge.

Patrick, R. (2017). Wither Social Citizenship? Lived Experiences of Citizenship In/Exclusion for Recipients of Out-of-Work Benefits. *Social Policy and Society, 16*(2), 293–304.

Petmesidou, M. (2014). Preface. From the Golden Age to the Age of Crisis. In G. Esping-Andersen, *The Three Worlds of Welfare Capitalism*. Athens: Topos (in Greek).

Pierson, P. (2011). Welfare State Reform over the Very Long Run. *ZeS-Working Paper*. Centre for Social Policy, University of Bremen.

Preece, D. (2009). *Dismantling Social Europe: The Political Economy of Social Policy in the European Union*. Boulder, CO: First Forum Press.

Sherraden, M. (2003). From the Social Welfare State to the Social Investment State. *Shelterforce Online*, 128. Retrieved from https://shelterforce.org/2003/03/01/from-the-social-welfare-state-to-the-social-investment-state/

Stockhammer, E. (2012). The Euro Crisis, European Neoliberalism and the Need for a European Welfare State. *Soundings, 50*, 121–130.

Streeck, W. (2014). *Buying Time. The Delayed Crisis of Democratic Capitalism*. London: Verso.

Turner, B. (2016). We are All Denizens Now: On the Erosion of Citizenship. *Citizenship Studies, 20*(6–7), 679–692.

Verhoeven, I., & Tonkens, E. (2013). Talking Active Citizenship: Framing Welfare State Reform in England and the Netherlands. *Social Policy and Society, 12*(3), 415–426.

Vis, B. (2009). Governments and Unpopular Social Policy Reform: Biting the Bullet or Steering Clear? *European Journal of Political Research, 48*, 31–57.

Wolff, R. (2010). *Capitalism Hits the Fan: The Global Economic Meltdown and What to Do About It* (2nd ed.). Northampton, MA: Olive Branch Press.

Woolford, A., & Nelund, A. (2013). The Responsibilities of the Poor: Performing Neoliberal Citizenship within the Bureaucratic Field. *Social Service Review, 87*(2), 292–318.

CHAPTER 6

Conclusions

Based on the preceding analysis, several important aspects of the transformations to citizenship and the welfare state in the preceding period can be identified. These transformations consolidate and give meaning to the aims, orientations and content of social policy in the two historical forms of welfare state examined (see Table 6.1).

The classification in Table 6.1 illustrates the aspects of the transformation of and transition from the Keynesian welfare state to the neoliberal welfare state. As it turns out, these structural changes are reflected in both theory and applied policies. The pages that follow will seek to summarize and compare these changes in order to reach a definitive conclusion.

Starting from the dimension of citizenship, the first component relates to the ratio of rights to obligations. In social citizenship, emphasis is placed on social rights, while in the responsible citizenship version it falls on individual obligations and responsibilities. In other words, the priorities go from being requirements to being citizen duties. In terms of identity, there is a marked shift from the aspect of class to the cultural lens of social inequalities. The focus is directed towards tackling poverty as a way of eliminating the exclusions that arise from cultural differences.

A catalytic development is the weakening of the concept of decommodification through the recommodification of social goods; in other words, the standard of living of citizens becomes even more dependent on market forces. Consequently, the transition from universal-type social rights to an individual fully funded system is an anticipated development.

N. Kourachanis, *Citizenship and Social Policy*,
https://doi.org/10.1007/978-3-030-59827-3_6

Table 6.1 Typology of transformations in citizenship and the welfare state

Social citizenship	*Responsible citizenship*
Emphasis on rights	Emphasis on obligations
Class identities	Cultural identities
Decommodification	Recommodification
Universal social rights	Selective social rights
Social needs	Social risks
Welfare	Residual support
Social cohesion	Extreme poverty management
Social responsibility	Social investment
Social participation	Inclusive society
Intergenerational solidarity	Individual capitalization
Keynesian welfare state	*Neoliberal welfare state*
Redistributive social policies	Residualized social policies
State social policies	Welfare pluralism
Holistic social interventions	Social innovation/Short term experiments
National delimitation	Supranational/Local delimitation
Recipients of universal social services	Selection of beneficiaries
Full employment	Flexible employment
Job-offer policies	Employability
Income-support policies	Active social policies
Cash benefits	Workfare
Redistributive pensions	Capitalized pensions

All these events go hand-in-hand with the structural shift of priorities from meeting social needs to managing social risks. The state's efforts to meet the social needs of its citizens are limited to helping prevent any fundamental challenges that may pose a threat to them. This shift coincides with the abandonment of the vision of civilized living, a shared intellectual heritage and the pursuit of welfare for a negative reorientation to the marginal management of extreme material deprivation. Thus, the aim of social cohesion is abandoned, to be replaced by the management of extreme poverty.

The legitimization of these changes in conceptual priorities has been instrumental in helping to restructure the framework of social responsibility. The most important development is the shift from social to individual responsibility, a parameter that runs through all the promoted changes. Its focus is the abandonment of state social responsibility and the development of a framework that promotes the individualistic concept of social investment; a concept that focuses not on collective responsibility to tackle inequalities, but on offering opportunities for individual empowerment and skills acquisition to self-manage social risks.

Focusing on one's responsibilities and skills legitimizes state withdrawal from dealing with social problems. Thus, any attempt to secure the social participation of citizens is replaced by a misleading aim for social inclusion. The aim is that citizens will coexist, regardless of the extent of their inequalities, and despite the fact that they have no prospects for social participation. This turns the right to be different into the right for inequality. Perhaps the most striking example of this response to the individualized landscape of citizens' social risk management is the change in the philosophy of the pension system.

These transformations in citizenship are in line with the corresponding restructuring of the welfare state. The main development can be seen as the reduction of its redistributive functions to the level of secondary income distribution policies and rights. This has occurred through an evolution that over the last five decades has led to a constant, albeit at different speeds, tendency for the residualization of social protection.

The shaping of this landscape of residualization has led to the privatization of social policy. In the new welfare mix, the state pillar has been weakened by the strengthening of civil society and the private sector, as expressed through welfare pluralism. This development is reinforced by the effects of globalization and, in particular, by social policy being made ever-increasingly on a supranational and sub-national level. Redefining levels of governance goes hand-in-hand with the weakening of holistic (and long-term) social interventions and the strengthening of short-term (and non-comprehensive) actions.

In the context of the privatization and the shrinking of state social policy, the introduction of exclusion filters for the beneficiaries of social benefits is to be expected. An increasing number of conditions are introduced in order for one to be eligible for social benefits, with the obvious criterion of focusing social assistance only on citizens who are on the verge of poverty. Indeed, this charitable conception of social policy is reflected in the replacement of the concept of the recipient, that is to say, the citizen who is entitled to social support, to that of the beneficiary, that is to say, the individual who benefits from a social contribution.

The reflections of these conceptual and ideological shifts in the areas of social policy intervention are manifold. From the concept of full-time employment and protected labor rights to a framework of flexibility in terms of both employment and labor rights. From labor supply policies we have moved on to employability policies. In other words, policies that oblige the individual to be able to work when there is a job opportunity. From income-support policies for the unemployed to activation policies, mainly through training and skills acquisition programs.

This is also manifested in the move from the payment of cash benefits because of the social risk of unemployment to forced labor practices for receiving social assistance (workfare). There are many other developments in different areas of social policy that illustrate this transition, but I limit myself to only one. The apparent tendency to move away from the redistributive pension model while favoring a fully funded model implies a shift from the value of intergenerational solidarity (that is, a value that promotes solidarity) to that of individual savings (that is, a value that prefers individualism). This is an ongoing process for the individualization of the framework of the standards of living, which is having a distressing effect on the increasing numbers of the socially disadvantaged.

Are the Keynesian welfare state and the Neoliberal welfare state two distinct historical forms, or is the former simply a historical parenthesis within a model of social organization that still does not serve the goal of dignified living for the citizen? The tendency for the disintegration of the postwar consensus occurred in a mild but methodical way during a prosperous state of affairs. It has accelerated abruptly and antisocially in the wake of the Great Recession of 2008, further spurring its shrinkage. Whether the Keynesian welfare state is something that is now only of historical interest or whether it projects images of a more social future will be answered by citizens themselves and their struggles.

References

Aasen, H. S., Gloppen, S., Magnussen, A. M., & Nilssen, E. (Eds.). (2014). *Juridification and Social Citizenship in the Welfare State*. Cheltenham: Edward Elgar Publishing.

Abel-Smith, B. (1958). Whose Welfare State? In N. Mackenzie (Ed.), *Conviction*. London: MacGibbon & Kee.

Abel-Smith, B. (1964). *Freedom in the Welfare State* (Fabian Tract 353). London: Fabian Society.

Abel-Smith, B. (1966). *Labour's Social Plans—Socialism Affluence* (Fabian Tract 369). London: Fabian Society.

Abel-Smith, B., & Townsend, P. (1955). *New Pensions for the Old* (Fabian Research Series No. 171). London: Fabian Publications Ltd.

Adriaansens, H. (1994). Citizenship, Work and Welfare. In B. van Steenbergen (Ed.), *The Condition of Citizenship*. London: Sage Publications.

Ajani, M. (2015). *Citizenship, the Self and the Other: Critical Discussions on Citizenship and How to Approach Religious and Cultural Difference*. Cambridge: Cambridge Scholars Publishing.

Alcock, P., Erskine, A., & May, M. (Eds.). (1997). *The Student's Companion to Social Policy*. Oxford: Blackwell Publishers.

Alcock, P., Erskine, A., & May, M. (Eds.). (2008). *The Blackwell Dictionary of Social Policy*. Oxford: Blackwell.

Alejandro, R. (1989). *Hermeneutics and Citizenship: Critical Reflections on Contemporary Liberal Theory and Communitarian Narratives*. Unpublished PhD thesis, Princeton University, Princeton.

Anderson, B., & Hughes, V. (Eds.). (2015). *Citizenship and Its Others*. Houndmills, Basingstoke, Hampshire: Palgrave Macmillan.

N. Kourachanis, *Citizenship and Social Policy*,
https://doi.org/10.1007/978-3-030-59827-3

Armingeon, K., & Guthmann, K. (2014). Democracy in Crisis? The Declining Support for National Democracy in European Countries, 2007–2011. *European Journal of Political Research, 53*(3), 423–442.

Barnes, C., & Mercer, G. (2003). *Disability*. Cambridge: Polity Press.

Bellofiore, R., & Halevi, J. (2011). The Great Recession and the Third Crisis in Economic Theory. In E. Brancaccio & J. Fontana (Eds.), *The Global Economic Crisis. New Perspectives on the Critique of Economic Theory and Policy*. London and New York: Routledge.

Bermeo, N., & Pontusson, J. (Eds.). (2012). *Coping with Crisis. Government Reactions to the Great Recession*. New York: Russell Sage Foundation.

Bernaciak, M. (2012). Social Dumping: Political Catchphrase or Threat to Labour Standards? *ETUI Working Paper 2012.06*. Retrieved from SSRN: https://ssrn.com/abstract=2208393.

Beveridge Report. (1942). *Social Insurance and Allied Services*. London: HMSO.

Beynon, H., & Nichols, T. (Eds.). (2006). *The Fordism of Ford and Modern Management: Fordism and Post-Fordism*. Cheltenham: Elgar.

Blackburn, R. (2008). What is Social Inequality? *International Journal of Sociology & Social Policy, 28*(7/8), 250–259.

Blakemore, K. (2003). *Social Policy: An Introduction*. Buckingham: Open University Press.

Bonoli, G. (2013). *Origins of Active Social Policy: Labour Market and Childcare Policies in a Comparative Perspective*. Oxford: Oxford University Press.

Brubaker, R. (1992). *Citizenship and Nationhood in France and Germany*. Harvard University Press.

Bruszt, L., & Vedres, B. (2008). The Politics of Civic Combinations. *Voluntas, 19*(2), 140–160.

Bulmer, M., & Rees, A. M. (1996). *Citizenship Today—The Contemporary Relevance of T.H. Marshall*. London: Routledge.

Byrne, D. (2005). *Social Exclusion*. London: Open University Press.

Cairney, P. (2012). *Understanding Public Policy*. Basingstoke: Palgrave Macmillan.

Cajaiba-Santana, G. (2014). Social Innovation: Moving the Field Forward. A Conceptual Framework. *Technological Forecasting and Social Change, 82*, 42–51.

Carmel, E., & Papadopoulos, T. (2009). Governing Social Security: From Protection to Markets. In J. Millar & R. Sainsbury (Eds.), *Understanding Social Security: Issues for Policy and Practice*. Bristol: Policy Press.

Carnoy, M., Castells, M., Cohen, S., & Fernando-Henrique, C. (Eds.). (1993). *The New Global Economy in the Information Age: Reflections on Our Changing World*. Pennsylvania: Pennsylvania University Press.

Clarke, J. (2005). New Labour's Citizens: Activated, Empowered, Responsibilized, Abandoned? *Critical Social Policy, 25*(4), 447–463.

Clarke, J., Newman, J., Smith, N., Vidler, E., & Westmarland, L. (2007). *Creating Citizen–Consumers: Changing Publics and Changing Public Services*. London: Sage.

Cohen, E. F., & Ghosh, C. (2019). *Citizenship*. Cambridge: Polity Press.

Copeland, P., & Papadimitriou, D. (Eds.). (2012). *The EU's Lisbon Strategy: Evaluating Success, Understanding Failure*. Basingstoke: Palgrave Macmillan.

Crouch, C. (2004). *Post-Democracy*. Indianapolis: Wiley.

Cutler, T., Williams, K., & Williams, J. (1986). *Keynes, Beveridge and Beyond*. London: Routledge.

Dahrendorf, R. (1994). The Changing Quality of Citizenship. In B. van Steenbergen (Ed.), *The Condition of Citizenship*. London: Sage Publications.

Dale, G., & El-Enany, N. (2013). The Limits of Social Europe: EU Law and the Ordoliberal Agenda. *German Law Journal, 14*(5), 613–649.

Danaher, K. (Ed.). (1994). *Fifty Years is Enough: The Case against the World Bank and the International Monetary Fund*. Boston: South End Press.

Dannreuther, R., & Hutchings, P. (2016). *Cosmopolitan Citizenship*. London: Palgrave Macmillan.

de la Porte, C., & Heins, E. (Eds.). (2015). *The Sovereign Debt Crisis, the EU and Welfare State Reform*. Basingstoke: Palgrave Macmillan.

Deacon, A. (2002). *Perspectives on Welfare: Ideas, Ideology and Policy Debates*. Buckingham: Open University Press.

Dean, H. (1996). *Welfare, Law and Citizenship*. London: Harvester Wheatsheaf.

Dean, H. (Ed.). (2004). *The Ethics of Welfare: Human Rights, Dependency, and Responsibility*. Bristol: Policy Press.

Dean, H. (2006). *Social Policy*. Cambridge: Polity Press.

Dean, H. (2007). Social Policy and Human Rights: Re-thinking the Engagement. *Social Policy and Society, 7*(1), 1–12.

Dean, H. (2014). A Post-Marshallian Conception of Global Social Citizenship. In E. Isin & P. Nyers (Eds.), *The Routledge Handbook of Global Citizenship Studies*. New York: Routledge.

Dean, H. (2015). *Social Rights and Human Welfare*. New York: Routledge.

Dimoulas, C., & Kouzis, I. (2018). Introduction. In C. Dimoulas & I. Kouzis (Eds.), *Crisis and Social Policy in Greece. Deadlocks and Solutions*. Athens: Topos (in Greek).

Dobrowolsky, A., & Tastsoglou, E. (Eds.). (2016). *Women, Migration and Citizenship: Making Local, National and Transnational Connections*. Florence: Taylor & Francis.

Dobson, A. (2000). Ecological Citizenship: A Disruptive Influence? In C. Pierson & S. Tormey (Eds.), *Politics at the Edge*. Basingstoke: Macmillan.

Dobson, A. (2003). *Citizenship and the Environment*. Oxford: Oxford University Press.

Donnison, D. V. (1975). *Social Policy and Administration Revisited*. London: Unwin Hyman.

Dummett, A. (1976). *Citizenship and Nationality*. London: Runnymede Trust.

Dwyer, P. (2000). *Welfare Rights and Responsibilities: Contesting Social Citizenship*. Bristol: Policy Press.

Dwyer, P. (2002). Making Sense of Social Citizenship: Some User Views on Welfare Rights and Responsibilities. *Critical Social Policy, 22*(2), 273–299.
Dwyer, P. (2004a). *Understanding Social Citizenship*. Bristol: Policy Press.
Dwyer, P. (2004b). Creeping Conditionality in the UK: From Welfare Rights to Conditional Entitlements? *The Canadian Journal of Sociology, 29*(2), 265–287.
Dwyer, P., & Wright, S. (2014). Universal Credit, Ubiquitous Conditionality and Its Implications for Social Citizenship. *Journal of Poverty and Social Justice, 22*(1), 27–35.
Edelman, M. (1988). *Constructing the Political Spectacle*. Chicago: University of Chicago Press.
Edmiston, D. (2017). Welfare, Austerity and Social Citizenship in the UK. *Social Policy and Society, 16*(2). https://doi.org/10.1017/S1474746416000531.
Esping-Andersen, G. (1985). Power and Distributional Regimes. *Politics and Society, 14*(2), 223–256.
Esping-Andersen, G. (1990). *The Three Worlds of Welfare Capitalism*. Cambridge: Polity Press.
Esping-Andersen, G. (1999). *Social Foundations of Postindustrial Economies*. Oxford: Oxford University Press.
Esping-Andersen, G., Gallie, D., Hemerijck, A., & Myles, J. (Eds.). (2002). *Why We Need a New Welfare State*. Oxford: Oxford University Press.
European Commission. (2010a). European Economy. The Economic Adjustment Programme for Greece. *Occasional Papers 61*. Brussels.
European Commission. (2010b). Europe 2020. A Strategy for Smart, Sustainable and Inclusive Growth. Brussels [COM (2010) 2020 Final].
European Commission. (2013a). Social Investment Package. Brussels.
European Commission. (2013b). Social Innovation Research in the European Union. Brussels.
Fahrmeir, A. (2007). *Citizenship. The Rise and Fall of a Modern Concept*. Yale: Yale University Press.
Farnsworth, K., & Irving, Z. (Eds.). (2011). *Social Policy in Challenging Times. Economic Crisis and Welfare Systems*. Bristol: Policy Press.
Faulks, K. (1998). *Citizenship in Modern Britain*. Edinburg: Edinburg University Press.
Feronas, A. (2013). *The Europeanization of Social Policy. Theoretical Framework, Methodological Issues and the Greek Experience*. Athens: Dionicos (in Greek).
Ferrarini, T., Nelson, K., & Höög, H. (2013). From Universalism to Selectivity: Old Wine in New Bottles for Child Benefits in Europe and Other Countries. In I. Marx & K. Nelson (Eds.), *Minimum Income Protection in Flux. Reconciling Work and Welfare in Europe*. London: Palgrave Macmillan.
Ferrera, M., & Rhodes, M. (2000). Recasting European Welfare States: An Introduction. *West European Politics, 23*(2), 1–10.
Ferrera, M., & Hemerijck, A. (2003). Recalibrating Europe's Welfare Regimes. In J. Zeitlin & D. M. Trubeck (Eds.), *Governing Work and Welfare in a New Economy: European and American Experiments*. Oxford: Oxford University Press.

Fine, B. (2012). Financialization and Social Policy. In P. Utting, S. Razavi, & R. Varghese Buchholz (Eds.), *The Global Crisis and Transformative Social Change*. London: Palgrave Macmillan.

Fitzpatrick, T. (2001). *Welfare Theory: An Introduction*. London: Palgrave Macmillan.

Flora, P., & Alber, J. (1981). Modernization, Democratization and the Development of Welfare States in Western Europe. In P. Flora (Ed.), *Development of Welfare States in Europe and America*. New Brunswick: Transaction Publishers.

Foucault, M. (1980). *Power/Knowledge: Selected Interviews and Other Writings (1972–1977)*. New York: Pantheon Books.

Fraser, N. (1995). From Redistribution to Recognition? Dilemmas of Justice in a 'Post-Socialist' Age. *New Left Review, 1*, 68–92.

Fraser, N. (2000). Rethinking Recognition. *New Left Review, 3*, 107–120.

Fraser, N., & Gordon, L. (1994). Civic Citizenship against Social Citizenship? On the Ideology of Contract-Versus-Charity. In B. van Steenbergen (Ed.), *The Condition of Citizenship*. London: Sage Publications.

Frericks, P. (2011). Marketising Social Protection in Europe: Two Distinct Paths and Their Impact on Social Inequalities. *International Journal of Sociology and Social Policy, 33*(5/6), 319–334.

Gaynor, N. (2011). In-Active Citizenship and the Depoliticization of Community Development in Ireland. *Community Development Journal, 46*(1), 27–41.

George, V., & Wilding, P. (1994). *Welfare and Ideology*. London: Prentice Hall and Harvester Wheatsheaf.

Geyer, R. (2013). *Exploring European Social Policy*. Oxford: Wiley.

Giddens, A. (1998). *The Third Way: The Renewal of Social Democracy*. Cambridge: Polity Press.

Gilbert, N. (2002). *Transformation of the Welfare State: The Silent Surrender of Public Responsibility*. Oxford: Oxford University Press.

Gilbert, N. (2012). Citizenship in the Enabling State: The Changing Balance of Rights and Obilgations. In A. Evers & A. M. Guillemard (Eds.), *Social Policy and Citizenship: The Changing Landscape*. Oxford: Oxford University Press.

Gilbert, N., Burrows, R., & Pollert, A. (1992). *Fordism and Flexibility: Divisions and Change*. New York: St. Martin's Press.

Gough, I. (1979). *The Political Economy of the Welfare State*. London: Palgrave Macmillan.

Gough, I. (1980). Thatcherism and the Welfare State: Britain is Experiencing the Most Far-reaching Experiment in 'New Right' Politics in the Western World. *Marxism Today*. Reprinted in LSE Research Online: http://eprints.lse.ac.uk/66525/1/Binder1.pdf

Gravaris, D. (1997). *Crisis of the Welfare State and Modernity*. Athens: Sakis Karagiorgas Foundation (in Greek).

Gravaris, D. (2008). The Social Content of Democracy. In M. Angelidis (Ed.), *Democracy and State Policy in Greece*. Athens: Sakis Karagiorgas Foundation (in Greek).

Gravaris, D. (2018a). Democracy and Social Policy in Times of Crisis—A Short Political and Economic Cycle. In C. Dimoulas & I. Kouzis (Eds.), *Crisis and Social Policy in Greece. Deadlocks and Solutions*. Athens: Topos (in Greek).

Gravaris, D. (2018b). Two Historical Forms of the Welfare State. In T. Sakellaropoulos, C. Economou, C. Skamnakis, & M. Angelaki (Eds.), *Social Policy*. Athens: Dionicos (in Greek).

Green, D. (1997). The Neo-Liberal Perspective. In P. Alcock, A. Erskine, & M. May (Eds.), *The Student's Companion to Social Policy*. Oxford: Blackwell.

Greenberg, E. (1981). Industrial Democracy and the Democratic Citizen. *The Journal of Politics, 43*(3), 964–981.

Gregg, O., & O'Connor, J. (1998). Introduction. Understanding the Welfare State: Power Resources Theory and Its Critics. In J. O'Connor & O. Gregg (Eds.), *Power Resource Theory and the Welfare State. A Critical Approach*. Toronto: University of Toronto Press.

Guven, A. B. (2012). The IMF, the World Bank, and the Global Economic Crisis: Exploring Paradigm Continuity. *Development and Change, 43*(4), 869–898.

Habermas, J. (1994). Citizenship and National Identity. In B. V. Steenbergen (Ed.), *The Condition of Citizenship*. London: Sage Publications.

Hacker, J. (2004). Privatizing Risk without Privatizing the Welfare State: The Hidden Politics of Social Policy Retrenchment in the United States. *American Political Science Review, 98*(2), 243–260.

Hacker, J., & Pierson, P. (2002). Business Power and Social Policy: Employment and the Formation of the American Welfare State. *Politics and Society, 30*(2), 277–325.

Hall, P. A. (2017). Varieties of Capitalism in Light of the Euro Crisis. *Journal of European Public Policy*. https://doi.org/10.1080/13501763.2017.1310278.

Hall, P., & Soskice, D. (Eds.). (2001). *Varieties of Capitalism: The Institutional Foundations of Comparative Advantage*. Oxford: Oxford University Press.

Hardiman, N., Araujo, J. F., MacCarthaigh, M., & Spanou, C. (2017). The Troika's Variations on a Trio: Why the Loan Programmes Worked so Differently in Greece, Ireland, and Portugal. *Discussion Paper*. Dublin: UCD.

Harvey, D. (2008). *The Condition of Postmodernity*. Cambridge: Wiley-Blackwell.

Heald, D. (1987). *Public Expenditure*. Oxford: Blackwell.

Heater, D. (1999). *What is Citizenship*. Cambridge: Polity Press.

Hermann, C. (2017). Crisis, Structural Reform and the Dismantling of the European Social Model(s). *Economic and Industrial Democracy, 38*(1), 51–68.

Heyes, J., Lewis, P., & Clark, I. (2012). Varieties of Capitalism, Neoliberalism and the Economic Crisis of 2008–? *Industrial Relations Journal, 43*(3), 222–241.

Heywood, A. (2005). *Political Ideologies*. London: Palgrave Macmillan.

Hill, M. (1980). *Understanding Social Policy*. Oxford: Blackwell Publishers.

Hill, M. (1996). *Social Policy: A Comparative Analysis*. London: Prentice Hall and Harvester Wheatsheaf.

Hill, M. (1997). *Understanding Social Policy* (5th ed.). Oxford: Blackwell Publishers.
Hochgerner, J. (2011). The Analysis of Social Innovation as Social Practice. In Zentrum für Soziale Innovation (Ed.), *Pendeln zwischen Wissenschaft und Praxis* (ZSI-Beiträge zu Sozialen Innovationen). Vienna and Berlin: LIT.
Hoffmann-Lange, U. (2015). The Impact of the Great Recession on Support for Democracy. *Taiwan Journal of Democracy, 11*(1), 53–78.
Hollanders, D., & Vis, D. (2013). Voters' Commitment Problem and Reforms in Welfare Programs. *Public Choice, 155*, 433–448.
Holmwood, J. (2000). Three Pillars of Welfare State Theory: T.H. Marshall, Karl Polanyi and Alva Myrdal in Defence of the National Welfare State. *European Journal of Social Theory, 3*(1), 23–50.
Hoxsey, D. (2011). Debating the Ghost of Marshall: A Critique of Citizenship. *Citizenship Studies, 15*(6–7), 915–932.
Huber, E., & Stephens, J. D. (2001). *Development and Crisis of the Welfare State.* Chicago: The University of Chicago Press.
Hviden, B., & Takle, M. (2017). Concept Paper for Activating Social Citizenship. *Report.* SOLIDUS Project, Deliverable 4.1, HORIZON 2020.
Isin, E., & Wood, P. (1999). *Citizenship and Identity.* London: Sage.
Iversen, T., & Soskice, D. (2013). *A Structural-Institutional Explanation of the Eurozone Crisis.* Paper presented at the Political Economy Workshop at the London School of Economics, June 3, 2013. Retrieved from http://www.people.fas.harvard.edu/~iversen/PDFfiles/Iversen&Soskice_euro2015.pdf
Iversen, T., Soskice, D., & Hope, A. (2016). The Eurozone and Political Economic Institutions. *Annual Review of Political Science, 19*, 163–185.
Iversen, T., & Wren, A. (1998). Equality, Employment and Budgetary Restraint: The Trilemma of the Service Economy. *World Politics, 50*(4), 507–546.
Jackson, W. A. (1998). *The Political Economy of Population Ageing.* London and New York: Edward Elgar.
Janssens, A. (1997). The Rise and Decline of the Male Breadwinner Family? An Overview of the Debate. *International Review of Social History, 42*(5), 1–23.
Jensen, P. H., & Pfau-Effinger, B. (2005). Active Citizenship: The New Face of Welfare. In J. G. Andersen, A. M. Guillemard, P. H. Jensen, & B. Pfau-Effinger (Eds.), *The Changing Face of Welfare.* London: Policy Press.
Jenson, J., & Saint-Martin, D. (2003). New Routes to Social Cohesion? Citizenship and the Social Investment State. *The Canadian Journal of Sociology, 28*(1), 77–99.
Jessop, B. (1991). Fordism and Post-Fordism. *Working Paper.* Lancaster Regionalism Group.
Jessop, B. (1993). Towards a Schumpeterian Workfare State? Preliminary Remarks on Post-Fordist Political Economy. *Studies in Political Economy, 40*(1), 7–39.
Johanssen, H., & Hvinden, B. (2013). Towards a Post-Marshallian Framework for the Analysis of Social Citizenship. In A. Evers & A. M. Guillemard (Eds.),

Social Policy and Citizenship: The Changing Landscape. Oxford, UK: Oxford University Press.

Johnson, N. (1997). State Welfare. In P. Alcock, A. Erskine, & M. May (Eds.), *The Student's Companion to Social Policy*. Malden, MA and Oxford: Blackwell Publishers.

Johnson, N. (Ed.). (2014). *Mixed Economies of Welfare: A Comparative Perspective*. London: Routledge.

Johnston, A., & Regan, A. (2016). European Monetary Integration and the Incompatibility of National Varieties of Capitalism. *Journal of Common Market Studies, 54*(2), 318–336.

Joppke, C. (2008). Comparative Citizenship: A Restrict Turn in Europe. *Law and Ethics of Human Rights, 2*(1), 1–41.

J-Pal Europe. (2011). Social Experimentation: A Methodological Guide for Policy Makers. Directorate General for Employment, Social Affairs and Inclusion.

Kalecki, M. (1943). Political Aspects of Full Employment. *Political Quarterly, 14*(4), 322-330.

Kallio, K. P., Mills, S., & Skelton, T. (Eds.). (2016). *Politics, Citizenship and Rights*. Singapore: Springer Singapore.

Keller Lauritzen, R. J. (2013). *Social Innovation in Local Government. Experiences from Denmark*. Danish Technological Institute.

Kerr, C. (1960). *Industrialism and Industrial Man: The Problems of Labour and Management in Economic Growth*. Cambridge: Harvard University Press.

Keynes, J. M. (1936). *General Theory of Employment, Interest, and Money*. London: Macmillan.

Kilman, A. (2015). The Great Recession and Marx's Crisis Theory. *The American Journal of Economics and Sociology, 74*(2), 236–277.

Kim, W. (2007). Social Insurance Expansion and Political Regime Dynamics in Europe, 1880–1945. *Social Science Quarterly, 88*(2), 494–514.

King, D., & Waldron, J. (1988). Citizenship, Social Citizenship and the Defence of Welfare Provision. *British Journal of Political Science, 18*(4), 415–443.

Kolberg, J. E. (2019). *Between Work and Social Citizenship*. London: Routledge.

Korpi, W. (1980). Social Policy and Distributional Conflict in the Capitalist Democracies. A Preliminary Comparative Framework. *West European Politics, 3*(3), 296–316.

Korpi, W. (1983). *The Democratic Class Struggle*. London: Routledge & Kegan Paul.

Korpi, W. (1985). Power Resources Approach vs. Action and Conflict: On Casual and International Explanations in the Study of Power. *Sociological Theory, 3*(2), 31–45.

Korpi, W. (2006). Power Resources and Employer-Centered Approaches in Explanations of Welfare States and Varieties of Capitalism: Protagonists, Consenters, and Antagonists. *World Politics, 58*(2), 167–206.

Kotsonopoulos, L. (2016). *The Lost Consensus. Welfare State, Capitalism and Democracy*. Athens: Sakis Karagiorgas Foundation (in Greek).

Kourachanis, N. (2018). From Social to Economic Citizenship. Reflections on the Transformation of the Welfare State. *Sociological Review, 5–6*, 157–180 (in Greek).

Kourachanis, N. (2019). Homelessness Policies in the Liberal and the Southern European Welfare Regimes: Ireland, Portugal, and Greece. *Housing Policy Debate*. https://doi.org/10.1080/10511482.2019.1641733.

Kröger, S. (2009). The Open Method of Coordination: Underconceptualisation, Overdetermination, Depoliticisation and Beyond. *European Integration online Papers, 1*(13), 1–22.

Kvist, J., & Saari, J. (Eds.). (2007). *The Europeanisation of Social Protection*. Bristol: The Policy Press.

Kymlicka, W. (2002). *Contemporary Political Philosophy: An Introduction*. Oxford: Oxford University Press.

Lalioti, V. (2018). Theories of the Welfare State. In T. Sakellaropoulos, C. Economou, C. Skamnakis, & M. Angelaki (Eds.), *Social Policy*. Athens: Dionicos (in Greek).

Lazzarato, M. (2011). *The Making of the Indebted Man an Essay on the Neoliberal Condition*. Los Angeles, CA: Semiotext(e).

Lemert, C. (2016). *Globalization*. London: Taylor & Francis.

Levitas, R. (1996). The Concept of Social Exclusion and the New Durkheimian Hegemony. *Critical Social Policy, 16*(2), 5–20.

Levitas, R. (1998). *The Inclusive Society? Social Exclusion and New Labour*. Basingstoke: Macmillan.

Lipset, S. M. (1960). *Political Man*. New York: Doubleday.

Lister, R. (1998). *Citizenship: Feminist Perspectives*. Basingstoke: Macmillan.

Lister, R. (2004). The Third Way's Social Investment State. In J. Lewis & R. Surender (Eds.), *Welfare State Change: Towards a Third Way?* Oxford: Oxford University Press.

Lister, R. (2009). *Poverty*. Reprinted Version. Cambridge: Polity Press.

Lister, R. (2011). The Age of Responsibility: Social Policy and Citizenship in the Early 21st Century. *Social Policy Review, 23*, 63–84.

Lowi, T. J. (1972). Four Systems of Policy, Politics, and Choice. *Public Administration Review, 32*(4), 298–310.

Lynch, J., & Rhodes, M. (2016). Historical Institutionalism and the Welfare State. In O. Fioretos, T. Falleti, & A. Sheingate (Eds.), *The Oxford Handbook of Historical Institutionalism*. Oxford: Oxford University Press.

Lynch, K., Kalaitzake, M., & Crean, M. (2018). Research Report on the Conceptualization of European Solidarity. Dublin: UCD.

Mahon, R., Boychuk, G. W., & McBride, S. (2015). Introduction. In S. McBride, R. Mahon, & G. Boychuk (Eds.), *After '08: Social Policy and the Global Financial Crisis*. Vancouver: UBC Press.

Manning, N. (1997). Social Needs, Social Problems and Social Welfare. In P. Alcock, A. Erskine, & M. May (Eds.), *The Student's Companion to Social Policy*. Oxford: Blackwell.
March, J., & Olsen, J. (1984). The New Institutionalism. Organizational Factors in Political Life. *American Political Science Review, 78*, 734–749.
Marinetto, M. (2003). Who Wants to Be an Active Citizen? The Politics and Practices of Community Involvement. *Sociology, 37*(1), 103–120.
Marshall, T. H. (1950). *Citizenship and Social Class*. Cambridge: Cambridge University Press.
Marshall, T. H. (1965a). The Right to Welfare. *The Sociological Review, 13*(3), 261–272.
Marshall, T. H. (1965b). *Social Policy*. London: Hutchinson University Library.
Marshall, T. H. (1969). Reflections on Power. *Sociology, 3*(2), 141–155.
Mayer, V. (2008). Crafting a New Conservative Consensus on Welfare Reform: Redefining Citizenship, Social Provision, and the Public/Private Divide. *Social Politics, 15*(2), 154–181.
McBride, S., Mahon, R., & Boychuk, G. (Eds.). (2015). *After '08: Social Policy and the Global Financial Crisis*. Vancouver: UBC Press.
McKeever, G. (2012). Social Citizenship and Social Security Fraud in the UK and Australia. *Social Policy and Administration, 46*(4), 465–482.
Mead, L. M. (Ed.). (1986). *Beyond Entitlement: The Social Obligations of Citizenship*. New York: Free Press.
Mead, L. (1997). Citizenship and Social Policy: T.H. Marshall and Poverty. *Social Philosophy and Policy, 14*(2), 197–230.
Milligan, C., & Fyfe, N. (2005). Preserving Space for Volunteers: Exploring the Links between Voluntary Welfare Organisations, Volunteering and Citizenship. *Urban Studies, 42*(3), 417–433.
Milligan, D., & Miller, W. W. (1992). *Liberalism, Citizenship, and Autonomy*. Brookfield: Gower.
Mishra, R. (1984). *The Welfare State in Crisis*. Hemel Hempstead: Harvester Wheatsheaf.
Mishra, R. (1989). The Academic Tradition of Social Policy: The Titmuss Years. In M. Bulmer, J. Lewis, & D. Piachaud (Eds.), *The Goals of Social Policy*. London: Unwin Hyman Ltd.
Mishra, R. (1999). *Globalization and the Welfare State*. Cheltenham: Edward Elgar.
Modood, T. (1992). *Not Easy Being British: Colour, Culture and Citizenship*. London: R.T. Trentham.
Moreno, L. (2016). Post-crisis and the Bronze Age of Welfare in Europe. *Working Paper*. Instituto de Políticas y Bienes Públicos (IPP) CSIC, Madrid.
Mthembu, S. (2015). *The Individual and the State: Between Libertarianism and Egalitarian Liberalism*. Unpublished MA thesis, University of the Witwatersrand, Witwatersrand.

Muehlebach, A. (2012). *The Moral Neoliberal: Welfare and Citizenship in Italy.* Chicago: University of Chicago Press.

Murray, C. (1984). *Losing Ground: American Social Policy, 1950–1980.* New York: Basic Books.

Murray, C. (1999). *The Underclass Revisited.* Washington, DC: American Enterprise Institute.

Murray, R., Caulier-Grice, J., & Mulgan, G. (2010). *The Open Book of Social Innovation: Ways to Design, Grow and Scale Innovation.* London: The Young Foundation.

Myles, J., & Quadagno, J. (2002). Political Theories of the Welfare State. *Social Service Review, 76*(1), 34–57.

Natali, D. (2010). The Lisbon Strategy, Europe 2020 and the Crisis in Between. *European Social Observatory No. 4.* Brussels.

Navarro, V. (1998). Neoliberalism, 'Globalization', Unemployment, Inequalities, and the Welfare State. *International Journal of Health Services: Planning, Administration, Evaluation, 28*(4), 607–682.

Newman, J., & Tonkens, E. (Eds.). (2011). *Participation, Responsibility and Choice: Summoning the Active Citizen in Western European Welfare States.* Amsterdam: Amsterdam University Press.

Nolan, P. (2011). Money, Markets, Meltdown: The 21st-Century Crisis of Labour. *Industrial Relations Journal, 42*(1), 2–17.

O'Brien, M., & Penna, S. (1998). *Theorising Welfare. Enlightenment and Modern Society.* London: Sage.

O'Connor, J. (1973). *The Fiscal Crisis of the State.* New York: St. Martin's Press.

O'Connor, J. (2002). Understanding the Welfare State and Welfare States: Theoretical Perspectives. In D. Baer (Ed.), *Political Sociology: Canadian Perspectives.* Oxford University Press.

Offe, C. (1984). *Contradictions of the Welfare State.* Cambridge: MIT Press.

Oliver, D., & Heater, D. (1994). *The Foundations of Citizenship.* London: Harvester Wheatsheaf.

Oosterlynck, S., Kazepov, Y., Novy, A., Cools, P., Barberis, E., Wukovitsch F., Sarius, T., & Leubolt, B. (2013). The Butterfly and the Elephant: Local Social Innovation, the Welfare State and New Poverty Dynamics. *IMPROVE Discussion Paper 13(03).* Antwerp: Herman Deleeck Centre for Social Policy—University of Antwerp.

Papatheodorou, C. (2014). Economic Crisis, Poverty and Deprivation in Greece. The Impact of Neoliberal Remedies. In S. Mavroudeas (Ed.), *Greek Capitalism in Crisis: Marxist Analyses.* London: Routledge.

Pateman, C. (2000). The Patriarchal Welfare State. In C. Pierson & F. Castles (Eds.), *The Welfare State: A Reader.* Cambridge: Polity Press.

Patrick, R. (2017). Wither Social Citizenship? Lived Experiences of Citizenship In/Exclusion for Recipients of Out-of-Work Benefits. *Social Policy and Society, 16*(2), 293–304.

Paul, E. F., Miller, F. D., & Paul, J. (Eds.). (2005). *Natural Rights Liberalism from Locke to Nozick*. Cambridge: Cambridge University Press.
Peacock, A. (Ed.). (1954). *Income Redistribution and Social Policy*. New York: Macmillan.
Peacock, A. (1960). *The Welfare Society*. London: Liberal Publication Department.
Perrin, G. (1969). Reflections on Fifty Years of Social Security. *International Labour Review, 99*, 249–289.
Peters, G. (2019). *Institutional Theory and Political Science. The New Institutionalism* (4th ed.). Cheltenham and Northampton: Edward Elgar.
Petmesidou, M. (2014). Preface. From the Golden Age to the Age of Crisis. In G. Esping-Andersen, *The Three Worlds of Welfare Capitalism*. Athens: Topos (in Greek).
Petmesidou-Tsoulouvi, M. (1992). *Social Inequalities and Social Policy*. Athens: Exantas (in Greek).
Pfau-Effinger, B. (2004). *Culture, Welfare State and Women's Work in Europe*. Aldershot: Ashgate.
Pierson, C. (1991). *Beyond the Welfare State?: The new Political Economy of Welfare*. Cambridge: Polity Press.
Pierson, P. (1994). *Dismantling the Welfare State? Reagan, Thatcher, and the Politics of Retrenchment*. Cambridge: Cambridge University Press.
Pierson, P. (1996). The New Politics of the Welfare State. *World Politics, 48*(2), 143–179.
Pierson, P. (Ed.). (2001). *The New Politics of the Welfare State*. Oxford: Oxford University Press.
Pierson, P. (2011). Welfare State Reform over the Very Long Run. *ZeS-Working Paper*. Centre for Social Policy, University of Bremen.
Pinker, R. (1974). Social Policy and Social Justice. *Journal of Social Policy, 3*(1), 1–19.
Pinker, R. (1980). *The Idea of Welfare*. London: Heinemann.
Pohlmann, M., Lee, J. H., & Yang, J. (Eds.). (2013). *Citizenship and Migration in the Era of Globalization: The Flow of Migrants and the Perception of Citizenship in Asia and Europe*. Berlin, Heidelberg: Springer Berlin Heidelberg.
Polanyi, K. (1944). *The Great Transformation*. Boston: Beacon Press.
Powell, M. (2002). The Hidden History of Social Citizenship. *Citizenship Studies, 6*(3), 229–244.
Powell, W., & Dimaggio, P. (Eds.). (1991). *The New Institutionalism in Organizational Analysis*. Chicago: University of Chicago Press.
Prasad, N., & Gerecke, M. (2010). Social Policy in Times of Crisis. *Report*. International Institute for Labour Studies, ILO.
Preece, D. (2009). *Dismantling Social Europe: The Political Economy of Social Policy in the European Union*. Boulder, CO: First Forum Press.
Procacci, G. (2001). Poor Citizens: Social Citizenship Versus Individualization of Welfare. In C. Crouch, K. Eder, & D. Tambini (Eds.), *Citizenship, Markets and the State*. Oxford: Oxford University Press.

Pufendorf, S. (1991). *On the Duty of Man and Citizen according to Natural Law*. Cambridge: Cambridge University Press.
Putnam, R. (1993). What Makes Democracy Work? *National Civic Review, 82*(2), 101–107.
Quadagno, J. (1987). Theories of the Welfare State. *Annual Review of Sociology, 13*, 109–128.
Ramos, C. (2003). *Globalization and Technology*. Manila: Rex Book Store.
Rawls, J. (1971). *A Theory of Justice*. Cambridge, MA: Belknap Press of Harvard University Press.
Rimlinger, G. (1971). *Welfare Policy and Industrialization in Europe, America and Russia*. New York: Wiley.
Rogne, L., Estes, C., Grossman, B., Hollister, B., & Solway, E. (Eds.). (2009). *Social Insurance and Social Justice: Social Security, Medicare and the Campaign against Entitlements*. New York: Springer.
Rose, N. (1996). The Death of the Social? Re-figuring the Territory of Government. *Economy and Society, 25*(3), 327–356.
Rostow, W. W. (1960). *The Stages of Economic Growth: A Non-communist Manifesto*. Cambridge: Cambridge University Press.
Rothstein, B., Samanni, M., & Teorell, J. (2012). Explaining the Welfare State: Power Resources vs. the Quality of Government. *European Political Science Review, 4*(1), 1–28.
Rubery, J. (1999). *Women's Employment in Europe*. London: Routledge.
Sakellaropoulos, T. (2018). Welfare State and Social Policy in a Historical Perspective. In T. Sakellaropoulos, C. Economou, C. Skamnakis, & M. Angelaki (Eds.), *Social Policy*. Athens: Dionicos (in Greek).
Sakellaropoulos, T., & Berghman, J. (Eds.). (2004). *Connecting Welfare Diversity within the European Social Model*. Oxford: Intersentia.
Scharpf, F. (2002). The European Social Model: Coping with the Challenges of Diversity. *Journal of Common Market Studies, 40*(4), 645–670.
Schmidtz, D., & Goodin, R. (1998). *Social Welfare and Individual Responsibility*. Cambridge: Cambridge University Press.
Sherraden, M. (2003). From the Social Welfare State to the Social Investment State. *Shelterforce Online*, 128. Retrieved from https://shelterforce.org/2003/03/01/from-the-social-welfare-state-to-the-social-investment-state/
Skocpol, T. (1984). *Vision and Method in Historical Sociology*. New York: Cambridge University Press.
Skocpol, T. (1992). *Protecting Soldiers and Mothers: The Political Origins of Social Policy in the United States*. Cambridge: Harvard University Press.
Spicker, P. (1995). *Social Policy. Themes and Approaches*. Edinburg: Prentice Hall.
Spicker, P. (2000). *Welfare State: A General Theory*. London: Sage.
Starke, P. (2006). The Politics of Welfare State Retrenchment: A Literature Review. *Social Policy and Administration, 40*(1), 104–120.

Stockhammer, E. (2012). The Euro Crisis, European Neoliberalism and the Need for a European Welfare State. *Soundings, 50*, 121–130.

Streeck, W. (2014). *Buying Time. The Delayed Crisis of Democratic Capitalism*. London: Verso.

Swenson, P. (2002). *Capitalists against Markets: The Making of Labour Markets and Welfare States in the United States and Sweden*. Oxford: Oxford University Press.

Taylor, G. (2007). *Ideology and Welfare*. London: Palgrave Macmillan.

Taylor-Gooby, P. (1994). Postmodernism and Social Policy: A Great Leap Backwards? *Journal of Social Policy, 23*(3), 385–404.

Taylor-Gooby, P. (2004). The Impact of New Social Risks on Welfare States. In P. Taylor-Gooby (Ed.), *New Risks, New Welfare: The Transformation of the European Welfare State*. Oxford: Oxford University Press.

Taylor-Gooby, P. (2008). *Reframing Social Citizenship*. Oxford: Oxford University Press.

Thompson, E. P. (1963). *The Making of the English Working Class*. Toronto: Penguin Books.

Tilly, C. (1984). *Big Structures, Large Processes, Huge Comparisons*. New York: Russell Sage Foundation.

Titmuss, R. (1958). *Essays on 'the Welfare State'*. London: Allen and Unwin.

Titmuss, R. (1968). *Commitment to Welfare*. London: Allen and Unwin.

Titmuss, R. (1970). *The Gift Relationship: From Human Blood to Social Policy*. London: Allen and Unwin.

Titmuss, R. (1974). *Social Policy. An introduction*. London: Allen and Unwin.

Townsend, P. (1975). *Sociology and Social Policy*. Harmondsworth: Penguin.

Townsend, P. (1979). *Poverty in the United Kingdom*. Harmondsworth: Penguin.

Tsoukalas, C. (2010). *Inventing the Alternative. 'Identities' and 'Diversities' in the Age of Globalization*. Athens: Kastanioti (in Greek).

Turner, B. (1986). *Citizenship and Capitalism: The Debate over Reformism*. London: Allen and Unwin.

Turner, B. (1997). Citizenship Studies: A General Theory. *Citizenship Studies, 1*(1), 5–18.

Turner, B. (2001). The Erosion of Citizenship. *British Journal of Sociology, 52*(2), 189–209.

Turner, B. (2009). T.H. Marshall, Social Rights, and English National Identity. *Citizenship Studies, 13*(1), 65–73.

Turner, B. (2016). We are All Denizens Now: On the Erosion of Citizenship. *Citizenship Studies, 20*(6–7), 679–692.

van Steenbergen, B. (1994). The Condition of Citizenship: An Introduction. In B. van Steenbergen (Ed.), *The Condition of Citizenship*. London: Sage Publications.

Venieris, D. (2002). *European Social Charter: The Social Policy of the European Council*. Athens: Ellinika Grammata (in Greek).

Venieris, D. (2006). Limits of Social Policy. *International Conference*, Faculty of Social Policy. Panteion University, Athens (in Greek).

Venieris, D. (2013). *European Social Policy and Social Rights: The End of the Rapsody* (2nd ed.). Athens: Topos (in Greek).

Venieris, D. (2015). *Social Policy. Concepts and Relations* (p. 303). Athens: Topos (in Greek).

Verhoeven, I., & Tonkens, E. (2013). Talking Active Citizenship: Framing Welfare State Reform in England and the Netherlands. *Social Policy and Society, 12*(3), 415–426.

Vis, B. (2009). Governments and Unpopular Social Policy Reform: Biting the Bullet or Steering Clear? *European Journal of Political Research, 48*, 31–57.

Walby, S. (1994). Gender, Work, and Post-Fordism: The EC Context. *International Journal of Sociology, 24*(4), 67–82.

Wallerstein, I. (2003). Citizens All? Citizens Some! The Making of the Citizen. *Comparative Studies in Society and History, 45*, 650–679.

Weir, M., Orloff, A. S., & Skocpol, T. (Eds.). (1988). *The Politics of Social Policy in the United States*. Princeton: Princeton University Press.

Weithman, P. J. (2006). *Religion and the Obligations of Citizenship*. Cambridge: Cambridge University Press.

Wilensky, H. (1975). *The Welfare State and Equality*. Berkley: University of California Press.

Wilensky, H., & Lebaux, C. (1965). *Industrial Society and Social Welfare*. New York: Free Press.

Wincott, D. (2006). Social Policy and Social Citizenship: Britain's Welfare States. *Publius, 36*(1), 169–188.

Wolff, R. (2010). *Capitalism Hits the Fan: The Global Economic Meltdown and What to Do About It* (2nd ed.). Northampton, MA: Olive Branch Press.

Woolford, A., & Nelund, A. (2013). The Responsibilities of the Poor: Performing Neoliberal Citizenship within the Bureaucratic Field. *Social Service Review, 87*(2), 292–318.

Wright, E. O. (2000). Working-Class Power, Capitalist-Class Interests and Class Compromise. *American Journal of Sociology, 105*(4), 957–1002.

Wright, S., Marston, G., & McDonald, C. (2011). The Role of Non-Profit Organizations in the Mixed Economy of Welfare-to-Work in the UK and Australia. *Social Policy and Administration, 45*(3), 299–318.

Yalcin-Heckman, L. (2011). Introduction: Claiming Social Citizenship. *Citizenship Studies, 15*(3–4), 433–439.

Yeates, N. (2001). *Globalization and Social Policy*. London: Sage Publications.